FALLEN HEROES:

SIXTEEN MASTER VILLAIN ARCHETYPES

Tami D. Cowden

:

DEDICATION

For all the fictional villains who so desperately
want their own stories told.

CONTENTS

A Note from the Author   i

1   Introduction   1

2   Male Villain # 1 –The Tyrant   11

3   MALE VILLAIN #2- THE BASTARD   18

4   Male Villain # 3 –The Devil   24

5   Male Villain # 4 –The Traitor   31

6   Male Villain # 5 – The Evil Genius   37

7   Male Villain # 6 –The Sadist   43

8   Male Villain # 7 – The Outcast   49

9   Male Villain # 8 – The Terrorist   55

10   Female Villain # 1 – The Bitch   62

11   Female Villain # 2 – The Black Widow   69

12   Female Villain # 3 – The Backstabber   76

13   Female Villain # 4 – The Lunatic   81

14   Female Villain # 5 – The Parasite   86

15   Female Villain # 6 – The Schemer   90

16   Female Villain # 7 – The Fanatic   96

17   Female Villain # 6 – The Matriarch   100

18   Exercise 1 – Character Motivation   106

19   Exercise 2 – Physical Appearance   108

20   Exercise – Perception of Other Characters   111

21   Exercise 4 - Introspection   113

22   Exercise 5 – Words and Deeds   115

A NOTE FROM THE AUTHOR

The book you have purchased contains the lectures and exercises used during the online classes I gave several years ago. My current schedule does not allow me to continue to give those classes, but I receive frequent inquiry about them. Accordingly, I decided to make the content from the class available in this form. The lectures here are as they were in the classes, with some cleanup here and there, a few changes due to the different medium, and a bit of updating of the examples.

Because most of my students were familiar with the book about hero and heroine archetypes written by Caro LaFever, Sue Viders and me, *The Complete Writer's Guide to Heroes and Heroines: Sixteen Master Archetypes* (Lone Eagle 2000), I often referred to it or to those archetypes. While you do not need to have that book to understand the Villain Archetypes, you might find it useful. It is available in both print and digital form. You can also find a description of the hero and heroine archetypes at my website, www.heroarchetypes.com

Thanks go out to Caro and Sue, with whom I spent more than a year laboring over the heroes and heroines, and who encouraged the development of these villains and to everyone who ever attended a workshop or online class, because I never taught one that did not also teach me something.

In this bold new world of publishing on demand and digital publishing, it is possible to put out new editions in the blink of an eye. The examples I used in my classes are still valid, but I know there have been hundreds, if not thousands, of great villains created by many writers out there. The more examples presented, the easier it is for writers to grasp the concepts. Please send me your suggestions for additional examples of these archetypes from movies or TV shows. If I use your suggestion, I'll include your name in acknowledgments.

Please feel free to write to me with any questions or comments you have to tami @tamicowden.com.

Meanwhile, write your villain with passion!

Tami

1 INTRODUCTION

What are Archetypes?

The word was coined by Carl Jung, who theorized that humans have a collective unconscious, "deposits of the constantly repeated experiences of humanity.... a kind of readiness to reproduce over and over again the same or similar mythical ideas...." This shared memory of experiences has resulted in a resonance of the concepts of hero and heroine that transcends time, place and culture. Jung called these recurring personalities *archetypes*, from the Greek word *archetypos*, meaning "first of its kind." The observations my coauthors and I made for *The Complete Writer's Guide to Heroes and Heroines: Sixteen Master Archetypes* (Lone Eagle, 2000) were that there are recurring character types who have starred in story after story, entertaining and informing the human experience for millennia. Review of myths, legends, fairy tales, epic poems, novels, and film reveals that the protagonist types who recur in these stories fall into sixteen distinctive categories, eight each for the heroes and heroines.

Shortly after that, I took a look at villains – and discovered there are also sixteen – eight male, eight female, archetypes for those.

Let me stop there for a second. "Villain." That is the term I use, but I use it with some hesitancy. That word connotes evil, wickedness – real bad stuff. And if you are writing suspense or thrillers, that may well be the kind of villain you want to create.

But not every story has a truly evil villain. Sometimes, the "villain" – or antagonist – is really more annoying than evil. Not a serial killer, just a thorn in the side of the hero and/or heroine. So if you're writing a lighter story that needs someone for your hero and/or heroine to overcome, without that someone being evil, that's just fine. Each of the villain archetypes we'll discuss can be the really bad, horrible, scary type of villain. But each can also be more of the pain in the neck kind of villain. And every kind of villain in between. So keep this mind as you develop villains.

This "class" will focuses on the sixteen villain archetypes. These archetypes are:

Male:	Female:
The TYRANT	The BITCH
The BASTARD	The BLACK WIDOW
The DEVIL	The BACKSTABBER
The TRAITOR	The LUNATIC
The EVIL GENIUS	The PARASITE
The OUTCAST	The SCHEMER
The SADIST	The FANATIC
The TERRORIST	The MATRIARCH

These archetypes are not my invention – they have existed for millennia. What I have done is name and describe them, and provide examples of the characters individually. The names, by the way, were chosen with a view to conveying something of the character in a word or two. Please do not be offended at the choices.

At his or her core, every well-defined villain is one of these sixteen archetypes – and this is so because each of these archetypes is based on a corresponding heroic archetype. If you take nothing else from this class – let it be this: The Villain is the hero of his or her own story. Because of these heroic underpinnings, the villain's personality can find its roots in the heroic archetypes.

The archetype tells the writer about the most basic instincts of the villain: how he thinks, how he feels, what drives him and why he chooses both his goals and his methods. The skillful writer, in turn, conveys these instincts to the readers or audience, who, knowing at a glance the character of this hero, settles down to watch the tale retold anew.

Please note something very important here –

AN ARCHETYPE IS NOT DETERMINED

BY THE CHARACTER'S ACTIONS!!!!

I am serious – what the character *does* is not the defining element. The defining element is **WHY** the character does what he does.

"Any archetype can do anything –

the question will always be why."

Repeat that a thousand times. Tape it to your computer screen. Deface the cover of this book by writing those words across it!

What that means is that I don't want you thinking you have to have four different archetypes because your villain does four things that are what those four archetypes does. Uh-uh. Not the way it works. WHY, WHY, WHY – always look for the answer to that question to determine an archetype.

The existence of these archetypes, by the way, does not mean that in all of literature, there are only sixteen villains. Members of the same archetypal family are not photocopies of each other. Villains within a single archetypes share a similar psyche, but they **are not** and **should not** be clones of each other. Archetypes are not stereotypes; they are not cookie cutters. They can be considered a framework, or even better, a lump of clay of a particular color and consistency. Use the archetype as raw material to create a full bodied character.

Now –the class itself.

First a "handout" lists the sixteen villain archetypes. This is for easy reference – I list the eight male, and another, the eight female villains, each with a short description.

Then each villain archetype is presented in a separate "lecture." I describe their general demeanors, common tendencies, likely childhood experiences and behaviors, and likely flaws and virtues. Then I give examples of characters who are members of the featured archetypes. I include both modern and classic examples, from literature, film, and television.

My goal in giving all these various examples is try to hit at least two or three examples that each students recognizes. Books are the least likely media to be common among you – I am more likely to find a movie or TV show that a majority of you have read, than I am to find a particular book that is as well known. That is why I give movie and TV examples (I always get asked that questions!).

And there are also exercises – never more than writing a few paragraphs - which will give you an opportunity to put what you have learned about the archetypes into practice. These exercises also have another purpose – exploring the motivation, as well as the four ways to show, not tell, characterization in your writing.

So here we go...

THE EIGHT VILLAIN ARCHETYPES

THE TYRANT: the bullying despot, he wants power at any price. He ruthlessly conquers all he surveys, crushing his enemies beneath his feet. People are but pawns to him, and he holds all the power pieces. Hesitate before getting in this man's way – he'll think nothing of destroying you.

THE BASTARD: the dispossessed son, he burns with resentment. He can't have what he wants, so he lashes out to hurt those around him. His deeds are often for effect – he wants to provoke action in others. He proudly announces his rebellious dealings. Don't be fooled by his boyish demeanor – he's a bundle of hate.

THE DEVIL: the charming fiend, he gives people what he thinks they deserve. Charisma allows him to lure his victims to their own destruction. His ability to discover the moral weaknesses in others serves him well. Close your ears to his cajolery – he'll tempt you to disaster.

THE TRAITOR: the double agent, he betrays those who trust him most. No one suspects the evil that lurks in his heart. Despite supportive smiles and sympathetic ears, he plots the destruction of his friends. Never turn your back on him -- he means you harm.

THE OUTCAST: the lonely outsider, he wants desperately to belong. Tortured and unforgiving, he has been set off from others, and usually for good cause. He craves redemption, but is willing to gain it by sacrificing others. Waste no sympathy on him - he'll have none for you.

THE EVIL GENIUS: the malevolent mastermind, he loves to show off his superior intelligence. Intellectual inferiors are contemptible to him and that includes just about everyone. Elaborate puzzles and experiments are his trademark. Don't let him pull your strings – the game is always rigged in his favor.

THE SADIST: the savage predator, he enjoys cruelty for its own sake. Violence and psychological brutality are games to this man; and he plays those games with daring and skill. Run, don't walk, away from this man – he'll tear out your heart, and laugh while doing it.

THE TERRORIST: the dark knight, he serves a warped code of honor. Self-righteous, he believes in his own virtue, and judges all around him by a strict set of laws. The end will always justify his nefarious means, and no conventional morality will give him pause. Don't try to appeal to his sense of justice – his does not resemble yours.

THE EIGHT VILLAIN ARCHETYPES

THE BITCH: the abusive autocrat, she lies, cheats, and steals her way to the top. Her climb to success has left many a heel mark on the backs of others. She doesn't care about the peons around her – only the achievement of her dreams matters. Forget expecting a helping hand from her – she doesn't help anyone but herself.

THE BLACK WIDOW: the beguiling siren, she lures victims into her web. She goes after anyone who has something she wants, and she wants a lot. But she does her best to make the victim want to be deceived. An expert at seduction of every variety, she uses her charms to get her way. Don't be fooled by her claims of love – it's all a lie.

THE BACKSTABBER: the two-faced friend, she delights in duping the unsuspecting. Her sympathetic smiles enable her to learn her victims' secrets, which she then uses to feather her nest. Her seemingly helpful advice is just the thing to hinder. Put no faith in her – she'll betray you every time.

THE LUNATIC: the unbalanced madwoman, she draws others into her crazy environment. The drum to which she marches misses many a beat, but to her, it is the rest of the world that is out of step. Don't even try to understand her logic – she is unfathomable.

THE PARASITE: the poisonous vine, she Collaborates for her own comfort. She goes along with any atrocity, so long as her own security is assured. She sees herself as a victim who had no choice, and blames others for her crimes. Expect no mercy from her – she won't lift a finger to save anyone but herself.

THE SCHEMER: the lethal plotter, she devises the ruin of others. Like a cat with a mouse, she plays with lives. Elaborate plans, intricate schemes; nothing pleases her more than to trap the unwary. Watch out for her complex designs – she means you no good.

THE FANATIC: the uncompromising extremist, she does wrong in the name of good. She justifies hers action by her intent, and merely shrugs her shoulders at collateral damage. Anyone not an ally is an enemy, and therefore, fair game. Give up any hope of showing her the error of her ways – she firmly believes you are wrong, wrong, wrong.

THE MATRIARCH: the motherly oppressor, she smothers her loved ones. She knows what's best and will do her best to controls the lives of those who surround her – all for their own good. A classic enabler, she sees no fault with her darlings, unless they don't follow her dictates. Don't be lured into her family nest – you'll never get out alive.

MALE VILLAIN #1
THE TYRANT

THE TYRANT: *the bullying despot, he wants power at any price. He ruthlessly conquers all he surveys, crushing his enemies beneath his feet. People are but pawns to him, and he holds all the power pieces. Hesitate before getting in this man's way – he'll think nothing of destroying you.*

The first villain we will address is one well known in a number of fiction genres, especially romance, suspense, and fantasy: the TYRANT.

The TYRANT is the dark version of the CHIEF. He is the seemingly all powerful force that is determined to maintain control over the hero and/or heroine. In fact, maintaining control – having things his way – is his driving ambition.

You've seen this villain in many a story. He is the father or brother who tries to keep the heroine away from the hero – he wants her to marry someone "better," which often means no more than someone of his own choosing. Or maybe he's the dictatorial father of the hero who tries to crush any independent spirit in his son. Maybe he is the uncle or cousin determined to maintain control over the inheritance of the H/H. Maybe he is the battering husband or boyfriend. Maybe he's the boss who can't stand any deviation from his view of how the business should be run.

Or perhaps his relationship is less personal to the hero or heroine. He is the cruel monarch or dictator who crushes any rebellion. He could be the leader of some malevolent force – a crime family, a drug cartel, a group of smugglers, the CEO of a corrupt corporation, or the leader of an invading army.

The TYRANT can fit any time, any setting. Ruthless men determined to hold fast to their power thrive regardless of century or location.

And the heroes and heroines who stand up to those powerful men gain the sympathy and cheers of readers.

Formation of a TYRANT

How is a villain created? Sadly, the very same experiences that create a hero can also create a villain. A TYRANT might well have been born into the lap of luxury, and reared to view the world as owing him homage. Or perhaps he born into a slum, and determined to make his way out regardless of cost to others or to his own soul. He might have witnessed his father striding through a crowd of fawning admirers, and looked forward to the day when the power was his. Or perhaps he saw his own father spat upon by more powerful men.

Regardless of origins, the TYRANT is motivated by a secret fear – fear of a loss of control. The central fear will be loss of control over his own destiny, but that may also manifest as a determination to control everyone around him. Now admittedly, the same could be said for the heroic CHIEF, but the TYRANT has, in effect, given himself up to that fear. Unlike the CHIEF, the TYRANT is controlled by that fear. That terror of losing control leads the TYRANT to cross lines that would likely stop a CHIEF.

So when looking to create a backstory for a TYRANT hero – think in terms of control. What did he see or experience to make control so important to him?

Weapons and vulnerabilities

The Tyrant's weapons make him a danger to the H/H.

GOAL ORIENTED - Give the TYRANT something to aim for and he keeps going until he reaches the target. Always focused on what needs to be achieved, he plows through projects faster than most people, zeroing on what's important and discarding the rest.

DECISIVE - Bring a dilemma to the TYRANT and within minutes he's come to a conclusion about the best way to handle it.

His vulnerabilities are what they use to overcome him.

STUBBORN - the TYRANT sometimes becomes so focused on the mission before him that he loses track of when a cause is lost. Obstinate to a fault, even when someone points out that the battle is over, he continues to fight.

UNSYMPATHETIC- The TYRANT is impatient with tales of woe. Heartless, he expects people just to get over it. And doesn't care if they don't.

DOMINATING - Being right can be a burden, especially when no one listens. Irritated when decisions are not made right away, the TYRANT responds by trying to yank everyone into his corner. He will bully people into following him.

PROUD - his belief in his superiority can lead him to grievous strategic errors; a blow to his pride can lead him to rash conduct.

INCLINED TO ANGER – no calm reflection for him. Decisions he makes in the heat of the moment may well lead to his downfall.

Behavior and examples of TYRANTs.

In a darker story, a TYRANT might kill or commit other heinous acts. Murder, if the victim threatens the TYRANT's position. Rape, as a demonstration of power. Theft, if the article in question contributes to the TYRANT's power. And so on. The greater the power held by the TYRANT, the greater the risk of horrendous abuse.

I generally do not care to use real examples for villains but I make an exception for the ones that offer historical/political examples. Think of the terrible stories we heard about **Saddam Hussein's** treatment of his enemies. Absolute power, by definition, has no check. And it is not uncommon for dictator types to develop paranoia about conspiracies against them. It was true of **Stalin,** who routinely purged his administrations of suspected traitors (to him, not the USSR!). Numerous other dictators fit this archetype as well.

Or consider **Henry VIII**. His determination to control who would rule after him led him to divorce a pious and faithful wife, and behead another who was most likely innocent of any crime save failing to give him a son. His need to control this issue changed the religious face of the world.

In fictional examples, consider **Khan**, from the Disney film *Mulan*. His need to conquer and gain control of China led to the death of thousands, if not millions.

Disney likes its Tyrant villains, giving us another in **Hades,** from the movie *Hercules.* His desire is simple—he wants to take over Mt. Olympus and rule both the heavens and the earth.

A movie example, albeit based on real life – **Ike Turner**, from *What's Love Got to Do With It* is depicted as having a desperate need to control his wife.

Many of the James Bond villains are TYRANTs . They want to take over the world and are utterly ruthless in their employment of complex schemes and many henchmen to do it.

Do you watch *It's a Wonderful Life* during the Christmas season? **Mr. Potter** is a TYRANT. Look at the control he exerted over the lives of others though his bank. And when the opportunity came that might destroy George, that thorn in his side, he grabbed up the money left by the absent-minded uncle without a second thought.

If, like me, you are a *Harry Potter* fan, then you know an excellent TYRANT villain. Voldemort wants to gain control of all the witches and wizards, and, in fact, the world.

Of course, sometimes you need a less threatening villain. Sometimes TYRANTs are content to control their little worlds, and need not kill to do so. This TYRANT might simply behave in a dictatorial manner – being obnoxiously controlling. A great example of a comic TYRANT is **Robert DeNiro's character** as the overly protective father in the Focker series of movies, starting with *Meet the Parents*.

Or consider **Christof**, in *Truman.* He was certainly willing to "kill off" characters in the Truman show when the actors threatened his control over the world he created. But his villainy was entirely legal (well, probably not really, but in the story, anyway).

Rico Bandello, the title character of *Little Ceasar,* expressed his motivation "Yeah, money's all right, but it ain't everything." Yeah, I'll be somebody. Look hard at a bunch of guys and know that they'll do anything you tell 'em. Have your own way or nothin'. Be somebody."

As you can see from the above examples, a TYRANT can be matched with different kinds of heroes/heroines. WARRIORS/CRUSADERS often face TYRANTs – the people's champion facing down the great threat to freedom is a favorite of old. But even in these few examples we also have a BEST FRIEND, a LOST SOUL, a BOSS and a PROFESSOR. Your choice of villain should not depend upon what type of hero or heroine you have, but instead, on what kind of antagonism will lead your H/H to the growth s/he needs.

Now on to male villain # 2 - The BASTARD

MALE VILLAIN #2
The BASTARD

THE BASTARD: *the disfavored son, he burns with resentment. He can't have what he wants, so he lashes out to hurt those around him. His deeds are often for effect – he wants to provoke action in others. He proudly announces his rebellious dealings. Don't be fooled by his boyish demeanor – he's a bundle of hate.*

First off, let me apologize to anyone offended by a word that some consider "bad." Perhaps it would help if I explain that, in a sense, BASTARD is meant literally.

No, I don't mean that every member of this archetype is of illegitimate birth. Of course, there are certainly plenty of stories out there where this villain is truly a bastard in that sense. But the common experience shared by all members of the archetype BASTARD archetype family is a feeling that he has been cheated of his rights – whether a birthright or some other entitlement.

The BASTARD is a BAD BOY pushed to the darkness. Remember that a common emotion of the BAD BOY is resentment? A burning feeling of rebellion against the unfairness that has been dished out to him? That's what boils over in the BASTARD.

This fellow is a popular villain in genre fiction. He is the one trying to wrest the fortune, family business, estate, ranch, whatever, from the recognized heir. He is the displaced selfish boyfriend, trying to win back the girl. He is the evil twin, striving to get the goodies he should have, but his brother got instead.

Of course, he need not be genuinely evil. Perhaps his "villainy" merely takes the form of complaints, petty pranks, snide remarks, or other displays of envy and jealousy.

A BASTARD is more likely to have some sort of personal relationship with the H/H than TYRANT but that relationship might exist only in the mind of the villain. He has a reason to hate the hero and/or heroine, but they might not know the cause.

Formation of a BASTARD

Just think of situations that likely lead to jealousy, envy and resentment, and you've created a backstory for the BASTARD.

Maybe he really is a bastard – the son reared in the hovel, but always within sight of the castle. He covets that castle and tries to wrest it from his half brother or sister.   Or perhaps he has merely been displaced in the affections of a parent – an older sibling of a child more loved by parents. He wants that love back, and discredits his brother or sister.

Could he be the second son – jealous of the attention his brother receives merely as a result of an accident of birth? Or maybe he just hasn't lived up to expectations, and so darkly schemes to show Dad what he's worth.   Another possibility -- the object of his love has spurned him, and he covets what he thinks should be his.

You can see by these examples that what makes a BAD BOY can also make a BASTARD. Jealousy and envy rule him.

s and vulnerabilities

The Bastard's weapons make him a danger to the H/H.

CHARISMATIC - The BASTARD can be tough and mean, but he's also filled with devil-may-care charm. That gleam in his eye lures the innocent into his web.

STREET SMART - A graduate of the school of hard knocks, the BASTARD is wise beyond his years.   No one will catch him unaware in a dark alley.

INTUITIVE - His instincts are finely tuned. Childhood beatings or schoolyard fights taught the BASTARD that survival hinges on being constantly aware of the people around him. He's quick to assess someone's motivation and isn't afraid to go with his gut.

His vulnerabilities are what they use to overcome him.

PESSIMISTIC - The BASTARD expects the worst from everyone. This can lead to incorrect assessments and decisions.

BITTER - The BASTARD never forgets. His idealism has been crushed. Now only resentment and animosity remain. He carries his grudge with pride.

VOLATILE - On the surface, this man appears to be in control, but he's very emotional, and the seething rage deep inside him erupts if he's pushed into a corner. The BASTARD tries to bury his emotions, but he can't always master the volcano of pain bubbling beneath the surface.

JEALOUS – this is his demon. It can lead him to act irrationally.

Behavior and Examples of BASTARDs

If you've taken any classes from me before, you know my love for the world of **Buffy, the Vampire Slayer.** Long time viewers known what a glorious BASTARD Spike was. And the show's wonderful writers gave us his backstory – Spike was once the sweet and maudlin William, who wrote bad poetry and loved in vain. When the unworthy object of his adoration threw his poetic offering in his face, he went out into the London streets to lick his wounds, muttering his wish to "show" her. And then he met up with the vampire Drusilla, who gave him the means to show his true worth.   And so he teased and taunted and flaunted all that he managed to take from someone else. And when it looked like Angel had taken Drucilla's affection away from Spike, he coldly plotted Angel's demise. (But he was gloriously redeemed by his love for Buffy, even though it too, proved unrequited.)

Did you see **Gladiator**? Commodus, the son of the emperor who want to give the empire to Maximus, was a BASTARD villain. Think about how he hated the man who found so much more favor in the eyes of his father. Think of what he was willing to do to ensure his own "rightful" inheritance.

Public Enemy was a classic gangster movie, showing the rise and death of petty hood Tom Powers. Sons of a brutal police officer, Tom chose a life of crime, while his older brother, the one who "always [caught] catch the breaks" chose the straight and narrow.

Khan is a popular name for villains. Khan, from **Star Trek II: The Wrath of Khan**, is another excellent example of a BASTARD villain. Always he emphasized a sense of entitlement – a sense that what was rightfully his had been wrested away. Note, too, how personal his rage was. He focused his wrath on Kirk – the man who had wrested away what had been his.

Two more good examples of BASTARD villains are shown in **Star Trek: the Next Generation**. Lohr, the android brother of Data. Dr. Soong loved Data best, and poor Lohr had the emotions to feel that rejection. And one of the Star

Trek movies, *Star Trek: Nemesis*, features a clone, created for no other purpose than to destroy the original. He hates the human whose clone he is, and the Romulans who created and then discarded him.

The **Spiderman** series of movies features on-again, off-again antagonist Harry Osborn, Peter Parker's best friend. Harry's father had often shown approval and fatherly affection for Peter, ignoring his own son, thus leading Harry to a continuing resentment toward Peter that frequently erupts.

Note the tendency of the Bastard to lash out not only at the one he thinks has displaced him, but also at those who rejected his love.

Now on to male villain # 3 - The DEVIL.

MALE VILLAIN # 3 –
THE DEVIL

THE DEVIL: the charming fiend, he gives people what he thinks they deserve. Charisma allows him to lure his victims to their own destruction. His ability to discover the moral weaknesses in others serves him well. Close your ears to his cajolery – he'll tempt you to disaster.

The villainous version of the CHARMER, the DEVIL is a man who knows the secret desires lurking within the hearts of his victims. He is able and willing to exploit those secrets.

The DEVIL is a popular villain, and he comes in many forms. When a story includes the devil in male form, he is likely to be a personification of this archetype. . He might be depicted with pitchfork and tail, sitting on the shoulder of his victim, whispering sweet temptations into a receptive ear, while warding off the more angelic good conscience perched on the other should. Perhaps he will be shown as Satan,

Lucifer, Beelzebub, or any of the other names for the devil – more than one story has him offering up a complicated contract for the purchase of a soul.

But while I named this archetype the DEVIL, a villain from this family need not literally be a demon. He could come in a much more prosaic form – the used car salesman, who promises that sweetheart of a deal. Or the con man. Consider the clichéd mantra of the confidence game – you can't cheat an honest man. That's because the DEVIL plays on the worst aspects of his victim's personality. Or maybe he's a seducer. (Years ago, I saw Tony Randall sing a song entitled "Have Some Madeira, M'Dear" – he was the very personification of a DEVIL villain, seducing a shy innocent into his bed.) In fact, "seducer" was a name we considered for this archetype, but the devil tempts.

Manipulation is the DEVIL's tool. Since he likes to think he is an innocent sort, he tends to set events in motion, and then step back to watch the pieces fall into place. But it is not the power of such string pulling he enjoys (although he might well be amused by what he sees!). Oh no, the DEVIL wants whatever he has led his victim to foolishly lose.

Formation of a DEVIL

We'll leave for theologians (or psychologists, depending upon your point of view) how Satan, *et al*, might have been created. Let's instead consider human versions of the DEVIL archetype. How does a little boy grow up to be manipulative and deceptive?

Well, you are an old hand at this now. You know that the very same sort of experiences that create a heroic character, can lead to a villainous one. So what makes someone grow up to be a user? Chances are, a childhood spent seeing how human frailties lead to disaster.

Did his father put bread on the table by exploiting the baser nature of others? Did he discover that a smile and a wink got him a better grade than putting in effort with the books? Did his mother sweet talk the grocer into giving her more than her money's worth?

Or did he see a smooth talking man persuade his mother from hearth and home? Did a fast talking banker steal his family's farm? Did his parents lose their savings in a get-rich quick scheme?

Someone taught the DEVIL how to win his way into the good graces of someone else. Your job as a writer is to figure who that was, and how it happened.

Weapons and vulnerabilities

The Devil's weapons make him a danger to the H/H.

CHARM – A DEVIL will be fun to have around, especially at first acquaintance, when he is likely to be at pains to please. Chances are, he has a good turn of phrase. While those who have gotten to know him well might begin to see the tarnished around the edges, the less discerning will remember how he made them laugh.

ADAPTABLE – he has no difficulty fitting in to his environment. This man is a chameleon. He insinuates himself into a situation, and just as easily, extricates himself. He is also able to go with the flow. If the ground seems to be crumbling under his feet, he quickly finds ways to build it up again.

SELF-CONFIDENCE – this man has great faith in his own abilities. He can face insurmountable odds, and still believe he will prevail.

PERSUASION – his ability to size up another person, and recognize their desires makes it all too easy for him to convince others to fall in with plans.

His vulnerabilities are what they use to overcome him.

IRRESOLUTE - This might even be considered a virtue, because a DEVIL's willingness to throw in the towel is born of pragmatism. He just won't waste his time on a truly lost cause – if he *believes* it is lost. Easy pickings are his goal, so if the hero and heroine show no signs of giving in, then he might just walk away. (Very likely muttering that he hadn't really wanted that particular prize....)

HISTORY - The thing about the DEVIL is, his victims tend to come to their senses. And while sometimes they are too embarrassed to reveal their foolishness, other times they go straight to the authorities. Chances are, the DEVIL has practiced his trade awhile, and therefore, he has a past. Sometimes, it catches up with him at the worst possible moment (from his point of view).

ARROGANCE – Confidence is a good thing – unless it is misplaced. And sometimes the DEVIL can have just a tad too much. He may well overestimate his ability to persuade, or his victim's willingness to be deceived.

Behavior and examples of DEVILs.

A relatively recent movie in which the villain was literally the DEVIL was *The Advocate*. Al Pacino offered the hero the world, and fully expected him to pick the proffered apple.

Another devilish example of the DEVIL – Jack Nicholson in *The Witches of Eastwicke*. Notice how they turned the tables on him – giving him his own back.

Other examples of the DEVIL as the devil himself include: *Oh God, You Devil*; *Damn Yankees; The Devil and Max Devlin.* And there was one an automobile commercial on TV now that shows the devil offering a man luxury and power, but the man is content with the luxury and power offered by his car. Once again, the DEVIL is defeated by his own overestimation of the lure of what he has to offer...

OK – here's a somewhat lighthearted twist on the DEVIL archetype. The plant in *The Little Shop of Horrors* could make dreams come true. All he wanted in return was a little blood. He made it seem so reasonable an exchange, too.

A little more serious, but every bit as deadly, was *The Talented Mr. Ripley.* Notice how his ability to change himself, to mold himself into something new, made his plan possible.

Notice too, that the line is fine between CHARMER and DEVIL – hero and villain walk closely together with these archetypes. A number of movies have CHARMER/DEVIL protagonist, and therefore the hero, but whose conduct would otherwise make them villains. *The Talented Mr. Ripley* might arguably be a hero (and indeed, he does appear in a number of additional books by the authors.) A light example of this anti-hero status – *Dirty Rotten Scoundrels.*

As a Highlander fan, I was quite disappointed in the movie, *Highlander: Endgame*. But the villain was definitely a DEVIL. He persuaded his victims to join him by playing on their individual needs and desires. In fact, any type of demagogue character – a cult leader, a crooked televangelist, and so on, will likely fall into this archetype. These people tend to want the riches they get from the power, rather than the heady sense of power itself. One way to tell the difference – will they lead their people to death (probably a TYRANT, possibly a TERRORIST) – or will they turn tail and run when the going gets tough?).

A great television villain that viewers loved to hate (in fact, that "love to hate" stuff is a clue to a DEVIL archetype!). J.R. Ewing from *Dallas* loved to manipulate others, pull their strings, and generally persuade them to reveal their worst possible sides. He definitely got a kick out of it.

And here's a very favorite villain – *Dracula.* Until recent years, vampires, when portrayed as villains, tended to fit the DEVIL archetype. **Buffy**, **Angel**, and **Forever Knight** have expanded attitudes in that regard, but Dracula is definitely a villain who charms his victims to death.

The "Rev." Harry Powell in **Night of the Hunter** is a DEVIL who openly hinted at his villainy. Near the beginning of the movie, this false minister says "Beware of false prophets which come to you in sheep's clothing but inwardly they are ravening wolves. Ye shall know them by their fruits." Of course, the DEVIL can and will quote scripture.

Now on to male villain # 4 - The TRAITOR.

MALE VILLAIN #4
THE TRAITOR

THE TRAITOR: the double agent, he betrays those who trust him most.   No one suspects the evil that lurks in his heart. Despite supportive smiles and sympathetic ears, he plots the destruction of his friends.   Never turn your back on him -- he means you harm.

A TRAITOR likes the hero and heroine just the way they are. That means he doesn't want them to change, to improve themselves, and definitely not to surpass him in any way.   The dark version of the BEST FRIEND is a particularly popular villain for romantic suspense stories.   Often, this villain really is the TRAITOR of either hero or heroine. In other words, he is the last person anyone unfamiliar with suspense story structure would suspect.

In real life, TRAITORs tend to be unassuming types – that actually helps them succeed. Who suspects Mr. Everyman? Who thinks that quiet guy wearing the sweater vest could have a secret life? And it is true in fiction, as well. TRAITORS are the mild mannered accountants quietly bankrupting companies with their embezzlements, the cops in Internal Affairs who are on the take, the agents feeding incorrect information to blow smoke in the eyes of their fellow agents.

Of course, a TRAITOR doesn't have to be the mole or double agent. There is a less threatening version of this villain, too. He is the safe choice, the same old, same old. He's the guy the heroine doesn't have take any risks for or worry about, and subtly encourages her from every taking any risks, from ever moving past her current life. The one who's always there when she needs him -- as long as she doesn't stray too far from where we are. The one who uses guilt or misplaced loyalty to keep others around him from growing.

Formation of a TRAITOR

What turns a BEST FRIEND into a TRAITOR? Well, lots of things could lead him to his evil ways.

It doesn't seem like a TRAITOR would have those horrific backgrounds that other villains might have. He fits into the community so well, a regular pillar on whom everyone relies. But of course, he could easily have been the product of some terrible home, and has pushed it all from him to create his contented life. But maybe someday something just shakes him up. He sees the hero or heroine drifting away from him, perhaps moving beyond their comfortable little life. That causes him to snap, and try to hold on to what they have together.

But just as often, a TRAITOR has a background as uneventful as his current life. A product of a sitcom-like family, perhaps he grew up to expect the same happy existence, where every problem is solved in 22 minutes plus commercials. Decisions might have been made for him, food just appeared on the table at the right time. It's a bit of a shock to him when he realizes that live is something that you have to make happen – and that his friends are willing to make it happen without him.

Weapons and vulnerabilities

The Traitor's weapons make him a danger to the H/H.

SEEMINGLY TRUSTWORTHY – The TRAITOR's greatest asset is the trust the hero or heroine places in him. For them, leaning on this man is easy because he's never disappeared or wavered. They've come to rely on him, and that is exactly what he is counting on.

EMPATHY – The TRAITOR is able to make others like him because he really is a likable guy. He listens. He understands. He might actually care. And no one thinks anyone they like is a villain.

His vulnerabilities are what they use to overcome him.

COMPLACENT - The TRAITOR is used to things going along OK. He can be a little too content with himself and the status quo, and not realize right away that the hero and heroine are on to him.

UNASSERTIVE - The TRAITOR is accustomed to letting others take action for him. That makes it hard for him to be proactive when things start going against him. What's more, he likely hates confrontation, and so will avoid any face to face showdowns if he can.

EXAMPLES AND BEHAVIOR OF TRAITORs

A perfect example of the mild sort of TRAITOR villain is seen in *American Dreamer*. (If you have not seen this movie, rent it right away – seriously. It is fabulous!) The heroine's husband is a stodgy, workaholic kind of guy who doesn't understand his wife's dreams of being writer. He just wishes she'd get her head out of the clouds. When her creative writing wins her trip to Paris, he seriously believes she'll understand that it just isn't a good time for them to go. Maybe next year.

Another great example is in *The Wedding Planner.* Justin Chambers plays the heroine's childhood sweetheart, earnestly hoping to marry Jennifer Lopez. He's sweet, he's adorable, and half the audience really wants him to win her love. He's just not the right guy, which makes him quite antagonistic.

Few things could be worse than being stabbed to death by someone who is trying to steal your wallet. But there is one thing – you could find out that the guy who killed you was only trying to get your wallet because your TRAITOR needed your password to steal money from the company you both work for. Oh wait, it CAN get even worse, because then you could watch that good friend of yours put the moves on the grieving love of your life, still trying to get the password he desperately needs if he is ever going to get the money he owes to some REALLY bad people. That's what happened in *Ghost*, where we had the creepy satisfaction of seeing what happens after TRAITORS get killed by waify widows.

One of the best romantic suspense movies ever made, in my opinion, is *The Big Easy.* Hero Remy is a mildly corrupt police officer forced to face the fact that there really is no such thing as "mild" corruption. He also has to face the fact that the murderous villains he's been trying to find are his own fellow police officers, led by his own stepfather, who raised him like his own son. It's not uncommon for everything to just get out of hand for the TRAITOR. He might not have intended things to come to this, but when push comes to shove, he is likely to try to save his own neck.

Dr. Richard Kimball had one advantage over the police when it came to figuring out who killed his wife. Since he knew he didn't do it, he knew there had to be a reason the one-armed man was in his house. That reasoning ultimate leads him to the discovery that his good friend had been altering the results of medical trials. The villain in the *The Fugitive* was yet another example of someone who didn't mean to have anyone killed. But once it happened, a little thing like a death sentence for his innocent friend wouldn't lead him to confess all.

One of Shakespeare's greatest villains is Iago, who serves as the **Othello**'s right hand man, even as he plots the downfall of the noble general. He uses his intimate knowledge of his friend's fears to engineer his demise.

Now on to male villain # 5 -   The EVIL GENIUS

MALE VILLAIN # 5
THE EVIL GENIUS

THE EVIL GENIUS: the malevolent mastermind, he loves to show off his superior intelligence. Intellectual inferiors are contemptible to him and that includes just about everyone. Elaborate puzzles and experiments are his trademark. Don't let him pull your strings – the game is always rigged in his favor.

This villain, the dark version of the PROFESSOR, was almost the "Mad Scientist," because, of course, that is one common example of this kind of villain. A particular favorite of the comic book crowd, the EVIL GENIUS is nevertheless found in all kinds of fiction. And AFI's number one villain – Hannibal Lector – falls into this archetypal family.

The EVIL GENIUS probably is, literally, a genius, or at the very least he thinks he is. A major motivation for this fellow's bad doings is proving that he is smarter than just about everyone else. He *likes* to show how smart he is. Proving everyone else is inferior – wrong when he is right - is a major driving force for this villain. Often, serial killers are portrayed as EVIL GENIUSes – or at least, the serial killers who leave elaborate clues and set up traps for the detective. And of course, playing a game like this is way of proving he is smarter.

But sometimes he has a slightly different motivation – the pursuit of knowledge itself, a scenario most often seen with the mad scientist version. However, even that villain can usually be counted on to mutter at some point something about how his colleagues will finally have to admit he was right all the time.

More comic examples tend to have dark imaginings of showing up all those jocks and cheerleaders who discounted their nerdiness in high school.

Remember that genius can take more than one form. High intelligence is perhaps most often the mark of the EVIL GENIUS, but some particular special talent or skill could also serve as the genius involved. Remember that an EVIL GENIUS will likely be proving himself the best at that particular talent or skill. Computer hacking, for example, or magic might be the form of genius shown by the EVIL GENIUS.

And remember that an EVIL GENIUS need not be a truly malevolent force. For annoying, rather than threatening, villains, the EVIL GENIUS can be the annoying fellow who always knows useless and arcane information.

He's the guy who always shows up everyone else. The kid who always has his hand up in class, and even reminds the teacher to assign homework.

Formation of an EVIL GENIUS

Given his motivation is usually proving how smart or otherwise talented he is, a very plausible backstory for the EVIL GENIUS is that his genius is unappreciated in some way. His theories and experiments are laughed at by other scientists, or he loses his funding. Or he is the class nerd that everyone picked on, while copying his answers from the test. Maybe his creative endeavors were silenced in some fashion. Maybe he just didn't learn to live comfortably in a world where he is smarter than most.

Weapons and vulnerabilities

The Evil Genius's weapons make him a danger to the H/H.

ANALYTICAL - This is the man who thinks before he acts. The EVIL GENIUS methodically takes apart a problem, assessing each piece of the puzzle until he's found the perfect way to put them back together. He refuses to be rushed and his conclusions are invariably correct.

TALENT – the EVIL GENIUS tends to be intelligent, but he could have genius of another sort. He really will have some exemplary skill, and he uses it to defeat his foes.

His vulnerabilities are what they use to overcome him.

INFLEXIBLE - The EVIL GENIUS is definitely set in his ways, and he isn't pleased at the prospect of changing. He's convinced that his way is the only way and can list fifteen reasons why that is so. Because he is so convinced he's right, he may be slow to correct any mistakes.

HUBRIS – the EVIL GENIUS is a smart guy, but there world is full of smart people. The EVIL GENIUS often doesn't believe there are any others. As a result, he can be genuinely surprised by someone who either figures out his plan, or comes up with a better one. Another problem that EVIL GENIUS has is that he tends to tick people off with his intellectual arrogance.

Behavior and Examples of EVIL GENIUSes

AFI chose him as number one, and few villains seem to strike fear in the hearts of readers as well as Hannibal Lector – a brilliant psychologist who is a serial killer. His ability to quickly come up with unexpected plans allows him to escape time and again. And he loves playing those psychological games with FBI agents.

In the comic book and movie versions of Superman, the archvillain Lex Luther always has those complicated plots to take over the world – and show up Superman. Just what it is he gets when he takes over the world is never entirely clear, because control doesn't really seem to be what he enjoys. No – what he likes is the planning and plotting.

Batman had a number of EVIL GENIUS type villains. One clear example – the Riddler. He liked to pay his games and leave his clues, trying to prove he was the smartest of them all.

The Usual Suspects tells of a complex plot by a criminal mastermind. The story is mostly told by one of his underlings, and an unwilling one at that, Verbal Kint, played by Kevin Spacey. This is a spoiler, and I apologize, but it turns out the story was mostly a tale woven by the mastermind himself – and guess who played him?

A perfect example of the mad scientist villain can be found in any of the versions of *The Island of Dr. Moreau.* He experiments with mixing human and animal DNA, resulting in grotesque mutations. His devotion to science is unswayed by the unwillingness of his human subjects to participate in the experiments.

Well, even though I am a member of the DNRC™, I have to admit that Dogbert (from the *Dilbert* comic strip) is an EVIL GENIUS. His contempt for the 'induhviduals' he tortures is well known.

Another comic villain – the Brain from *Pinky and the Brain*. He's another one whose *stated* goal is to take over the world from the ignoramuses currently running it, but has he planned for anything after that. Nope. He just likes planning to take over the world.

Sherlock Holmes, the brilliant example of the PROFESSOR archetype, had as his adversary an equally brilliant example of the EVIL GENIUS. Professor Moriarity loved to match wits with Holmes, ever striving to prove himself the intellectual superior.

Now on to male villain # 6 - The SADIST

MALE VILLAIN # 6
THE SADIST

THE SADIST: *the savage predator, he enjoys cruelty for its own sake. Violence and psychological brutality are games to this man; and he plays those games with daring and skill. Run, don't walk, away from this man – he'll tear out your heart, and laugh while doing it.*

This villain, the dark version of the SWASHBUCKLER, was the hardest to name. The name "SADIST" certainly fits the bill for the most evil versions of this villain. Hurting people for the thrill of it is, quite obviously, exactly what a sadist does. This guy is the thug who gets off on other people's pain, who enjoys instilling fear in others. He might be the criminal on the crime spree, the serial killer who feeds on victim's last terrorized minutes, or the rapist who delights in the screams and whimpers of his victims. This version of the SADIST gets his jollies from the devastation he creates.

But the less horrifying version of this villain is a man we've all met, and yet don't run to dial 911 to report. He also is a thrill seeker, but it is not the pain of his victims that gives him the thrill. Instead, he simply enjoys pleasure for its own sake, and he places his own pleasure before all other considerations, including how taking his pleasure might hurt others. This version of the SADIST is not terrifying, but he can still be quite the villain, and the pain he causes it every bit as real. He's the guy who loves the thrill of the chase, but loses interests once he's "caught" the girl. He's the boyfriend or husband who constantly cheats because he "just loves women." He's the guy at the office who blows off the big project to go fishing. He spends the mortgage money on a big screen TV so he and the boys can watch the big game, he loses the grocery money in a poker game, he forgets about Valentine's Day, anniversaries, and the heroine's birthday because the boys invited him to go out for a few drinks. Face it – when it comes to romance, this guy is the very worst villain of all! So SADIST, it is.

Formation of a SADIST

More than a few doctoral dissertations have been written to explain the origins of vicious sadists. Use your imagination to create the horrific childhood that resulted in the brute. Parents who were as sadistic or more so, cruel guardians who savaged him, a life lived on the streets without receiving a single act of kindness. Perhaps he fell victim to one such as himself. Did he manage to escape with only mental scars? For those who like the paranormal, is he possessed of a demon of some sort? Any of these back stories could lead to the SADIST.

Of course, a less horrific background will suffice for the SADIST who eschews responsibility. Perhaps he had parents who never expected him to take responsibility for his actions. Did his aristocratic father keep him from ever taking any role in the administration of the estate? Perhaps he had wealthy parents who never asked him to earn his pleasures. Or maybe the opposite was true. Perhaps he was worked so hard as a child, he vowed never to lift a finger once he escaped the family home. Maybe he watched his father work himself into the grave, and he's determined to live life to the fullest now.

Weapons and vulnerabilities

The Sadist's weapons make him a danger to the H/H.

FEARLESS - The SADIST never hesitates when faced with danger. He doesn't freeze when faced with a gun or run away from the gang that's attacking him. He delights in finding creative ways to outsmart his opponent.

UNPREDICTABLE - The SADIST may go where the action takes him. Chances encounters may lead him down a different path, making it harder for the hero and heroine to anticipate and head off his next move.

His vulnerabilities are what they use to overcome him.

HOTHEADED - When a new adventure beckons, the SADIST rushes in where angels fear to tread. Imprudent in his excitement, he just might forget to weigh the danger before acting, which can make it a bit easier for the hero and heroine to foil his plan.

SELFISH – The SADIST can be lured with offers of alternative pleasures. His live-for-the-moment attitude often means he can be distracted from his goal. The restless energy surging through him is more important than anything else.

EXAMPLES AND BEHAVIOR OF SADISTs

The sheer opportunistic quality of a SADIST makes it difficult to guard against them. The moon shining villains in *Deliverance* hadn't set out to find a couple of weekend sportsmen to torment. But they didn't hesitate to grab the opportunity when it presented itself.

A nice example of the jerky sort of SADIST is found in Hugh Grant's character in *Bridget Jones' Diary.* He seduces Bridget, strings her along, drops her, and then wants her again when he realizes she no longer wants him. The thrill of the chase is what he is after.

In a movie filled with villains, the SADIST is likely to be particularly memorable. "Mr. Blonde" in *Reservoir Dogs* takes savage pleasure in his torment of his captive.

Mickey Knox, the villain in *Natural Born Killers,* offers a chilling vision of the random brutality of which a SADIST can be capable.

I mentioned one of my favorite classic films before. **Arsenic & Old Lace** features the hapless Cary Grant surrounded by his insane family. His LUNATIC (Female villain #5) aunts lovingly murdered homeless men, but, believe it or not, he had an even more frightening brother. Villain Jonathan Brewster was very upset about having been placed in an institution for the criminally insane, and now that he had escaped, he was determined to get even with his poor sane brother. Peter Lorre, as the reluctant doctor who would actually administer the torture is wonderfully amusing, slipping in hints of Jonathan's brutal past "No, please, Jonathan, not that [method of killing] again. That one was so horrible. Ohhhhhh."

More than one Roman emperor went down in history as being more interested in pleasure than in ruling the empire. *Caligula*'s excesses earned him a movie that had an all star cast (take my advice, and see the R rated version, not the X rated that the real stars weren't told about when they made the film!). Because Caligula was an autocrat in every sense of the word, he might be mistaken for a TYRANT. But his desire for power did not seem to be for its own sake, and he certainly did not have any real ideas about how the empire might best be run. He enjoyed his power because it allowed him to amuse himself as he pleased. It pleased him to torture others.

Remember Alex DeLarge (before the treatment) in *A Clockwork Orange.* A teen on a rampage, he and his gang brutalized others for the sport of it.

The late Heath Ledger took Alex DeLarge as one of his role models for the role of the Joker in *The Dark Knight*. The ever-smiling face never showed such malevolence before that portrayal.

Next, Male Villain #7 – The OUTCAST

MALE VILLAIN #7
THE OUTCAST

THE OUTCAST: the lonely outsider, he wants desperately to belong. Tortured and unforgiving, he has been set off from others, and usually for good cause. He craves redemption, but is willing to gain it by sacrificing others. Waste no sympathy on him - he'll have none for you.

The OUTCAST villain is that poor soul who lives on the fringes – fringes of society, fringes of the neighborhood, fringes of the workplace. In mysteries from the 30's, the various suspects always put forth the OUTCAST as the villain – the hermit who keeps to himself, or the murderous tramp who wandered into the otherwise happy home to kill the rich lord who just happened to be about to change his will. Of course, the random stranger killer is a rarely a successful or believable type of villain, and so when the OUTCAST really is the villain, rather than convenient scapegoat, he tends to be a bit more complex – and much less obvious.

The OUTCAST is an increasingly common villain, because he often offers a psychological complexity. What's more, this villain might easily evoke sympathy, because he tends to be motivated by a desire to be accepted, to be loved, to be part of the group.

So he might be the rejected boyfriend, who goes to extremes to win the love of the object of his desire. Terrifying as they may be, a typical stalker really does want love. (Beware, however, an abusive boyfriend or husband might stalk their wife/girlfriend, but wants control, not love.)

An OUTCAST can give the readers the creeps, even if he has no malevolent intent. So remember that even if you don't need actual mayhem in your story, you can add a bit of conflict by having the guy at work who stares at the heroine a bit too much, or whose poor social skills lead to embarrassing moments for the heroine. This type of character, too, can evoke sympathy all too easily, so make him unrepentant of the distress he causes, however unwittingly.

Formation of a OUTCAST

Yep, it is true here, too. The little boy could have grown up to be a LOST SOUL, but instead, whatever happened in his life turned him into an OUTCAST.

Something set him apart from others. Something made him feel alone, unloved, probably unlovable. Psychological problems are just one possibility. An illness, a disfigurement, a parent who alienated others in the neighborhood – all might lead to the OUTCAST personality.

Or perhaps someone deliberately set out to make him feel that way. Abusive parents come in many forms. Physical abuse might leave psychological scars; constantly belittlement almost certainly will.

Or maybe he has certain desires or tendencies that isolate him from society. Even if he is able to disguise his desires, the pedophile is the very epitome of the OUTCAST. He cannot reveal his true self, even if he does not act on his urges, for fear of public shunning.

Weapons and vulnerabilities

The Outcast's weapons make him a danger to the H/H.

DEDICATED - the OUTCAST gives everything to what he believes in, holding back nothing. When he makes a commitment, he gives his all. His unwillingness to give up means the hero and heroine must be vigilant.

ASTUTE - there are no secrets kept from the OUTCAST. He's able to see beneath the surface, straight to the core. Because he sits apart from the world, watching and listening, he's able to judge people's motivations with astounding accuracy.

His vulnerabilities are what they use to overcome him.

INTOLERANT - his sense of idealism trips him up, with others and even with himself. He expects perfection and has a hard time grasping that everyone has faults. The OUTCAST can't seem to forget the offenses done to him. Frustration fills his life.

DEFEATIST - he wishes for the best, but the OUTCAST anticipates the worst He immediately sees the negatives in people and knows they won't change. Catastrophe is around every corner and he resigns himself to the whims of fate.

THIN SKINNED - the OUTCAST is easily hurt. He feels deeply, whether he admits it or not. Criticism and censure slash deep wounds into his soul.

Behavior and examples of OUTCASTs.

The LOST SOUL/OUTCAST archetypes also tend to have a lot of crossover type characters. Hero? Villain? Sometimes you only know by how it ends. If the outcast character lives and gets the girl, then he's the hero. If the girl ends up with someone else, and the outcast is dead, then he's a villain, however misunderstood. Put another way, if Beast gets Beauty, he's a heroic LOST SOUL. If not, he's a villainous OUTCAST. (If the girl dies, too, then, of course, you have literary fiction, and a tragic hero. See *Hamlet*. <g>)

King Kong – the romance here was definitely doomed from the start, but poor Kong still had to try his luck. He might have been a nice ape if left to his own devices, but once he set his sights on Fay Wray, he had to be defeated.

Phantom of the Opera – again, you have some sympathy for the tragedy of this character, but his willingness to gain his ends by deception makes him a villain. Blackmail and extortion were tools he was willing to use. He was redeemed in the end, but still had to pay for past crimes.

American Beauty –Self loathing is one sure signs of an OUTCAST. The villain in this movie despises his own homosexual urges. When he acts upon them, only to be rejected, he must destroy the person who knows his secret.

Judd in *Oklahoma* – imagine being the sort of person whom others urge to suicide! "Poor Judd is Dead" is a favorite song from this show, and is all about Curly's efforts (in typical CHARMER FASHION!) to urge Judd to do himself in. Judd is the type of person who makes the flesh crawl, and he knows it. When Laurey doesn't respond to his overtures, he is prepared to take what he wants by force.

Norman Bates from *Psycho*. Now, do not make the mistake of thinking that crazy automatically mean OUTCAST. But it can help. Being crazy prevents you from getting close to others (or others getting close to you.) And so, in one's loneliness, one might just to develop a fantasy of someone who loves you a little too much....

A classic example – *Richard III* (Shakespeare, not the real thing!). " Okay, he is really the protagonist, and thus, technically not a villain, but if you think of Henry IV as the hero, then Richard is a villain. Everyone adores his older brother ("this glorious sun of York" – who was also a son of York), but everyone despises the deformed Richard, even his own mother. "Since I cannot prove a lover . . . I am determined to prove a villain."

If you've seen the musical version of *The Scarlet Pimpernel*, then you have seen a fabulous OUTCAST villain. A single line defines the character. Near the end, when he taunts Marguerite that she will die alone, she replies, "It is you who are alone." Her rejection of him colors his entire world view.

Heroic characters like redeeming OUTCASTS. So if you want a story where all ends well, consider this example: *Rudolph, The Red Nosed Reindeer*, with his dentist friend, turns the vicious Abominable Snowman into a helpful hand around the toyshop. Another example – *The Grinch Who Stole Christmas.* And a not so cute example? Travis Bickle, from *Taxi Driver.*

One more male villain to go – male villain #8.

MALE VILLAIN #8
THE TERRORIST

THE TERRORIST: *the dark knight, he serves a warped code of honor. Self-righteous, he believes in his own virtue, and judges all around him by a strict set of laws. The end will always justify his nefarious means, and no conventional morality will give him pause. Don't try to appeal to his sense of justice – his justice does not resemble yours.*

We are much too familiar with this type of villain today, as far too many real examples exist in real life. Of course, all villains resemble real life personalities. However, please remember that the names of the archetypes are chosen simply for their ability to connote the archetype in as few words as possible. A character of the TERRORIST archetype family may literally be a terrorist, but it is the zealous mindset typically shared by such villains that is ultimately determines the archetype. A TERRORIST villain is motivated by a rigid adherence to his beliefs or cause. In fact, a character might literally be a terrorist in the story, but the motivation for his villainy could place the character in a different archetypal family.

In fiction, the TERRORIST has long been a popular villain. As I said, the character is literally a terrorist – Tom Clancy has written many books requiring Jack Ryan to overcome such villains. Suzanne Brockmann has a series about men whose daily job is to fight these villains. The list of authors who have written TERRORIST villains could go on forever.

Of course, the TERRORIST villain need not literally be devoted to creating terror in the hearts of citizenry, in furtherance of some political cause. Perhaps the villain has singled out a victim due to a personal grudge or a desire for revenge. Or the TERRORIST villain could be loyal to some force in opposition to the hero/heroine – the opposing army or the invading force from another planet. The German officer who remains loyal to the Nazi Fatherland (or the British officer during revolutionary times, or the French officer during the Napoleonic Wars, and so on) may not fit our view of terrorist as we understand the word today, but from the perspective of the Allied/American/British hero or heroine, that officer is a TERRORIST villain.

Of course, a TERRORIST villain may be completely nonviolent. We've all seen movies or read stories where a police captain or army officer or some high uppity up always insists on playing by the rules, even though the hero/heroine might be better served by bending them now and again. Think of how the cop who does everything by the book, gets in the way of the H/H who stretches things. Consider how annoying is the kid who always runs to tell the teacher of even *potential* infraction of rules. Or think of the rigidly moralistic type who frowns on any type of pleasure. These types won't blow up any buildings, but they can place obstacles in the path of the hero or heroine.

And, ultimately, fictional villainy is about placing obstacles in the path of the hero and heroine. What makes the TERRORIST villain (and his sister archetype, the FANATIC) particularly good in a story is the fact that sometimes readers do give that grudging sympathy for that "true" cause.

Formation of a TERRORIST

The nature of the TERRORIST can makes back story unusually uncomplicated. If the cause if political, then sometimes just growing up in places where oppression by the "other side" exists goes a long way toward establishing the back story. Sometimes, hatred is actively taught. Long ago, I read about a sign in the midst of a particularly strife-ridden neighborhood in Ireland that read, "If you were raised as they were raised, and taught as they were taught, you'd believe what they believe." A TERRORIST might well be the product of a family or school atmosphere that promoted the kind of hatred for whomever is on the other side. Often, we don't question what is presented as truth to us as children.

What's more, any war-torn atmosphere breeds proponents for both war and peace, with or without teachers actively promoting one side or another. Even those who want to continue the hostilities tend to believe, or at least, hope, that some definitive battle will lead to victory of their side, and then, finally, peace.

But a TERRORIST need not be that simply formed. Sometimes, the cause might only be perception, rather than actual wrongs done by one group. A father's job lost because "they" – fill in the blank: immigrants, women, members of other races – are taking away the jobs. A family's business or farm lost because of a perception of fraudulent banking practices. Rules were broken, and someone died as a result. Some sort of loss may occur, and the villain fixates on a reason that may, or may not, be true.

As ever, any of these causes could form a hero - the TERRORIST is the dark version of a WARRIOR.

Weapons and vulnerabilities

The Terrorist's weapons make him a danger to the H/H.

INCORRUPTIBLE - The TERRORIST holds fast to his ideals. He will not be lured from the path his just path by offers of riches, women, or other things that might tempt lesser men.

SINCERE - Make no mistake – he will not act against another based on mere hypocrisy intended to serve his own ends. He honestly believes his accusations, which makes him all the better at persuading others.

His vulnerabilities are what they use to overcome him.

IDEALIST – the TERRORIST will be buoyed up by his faith. As long as he believes, he will not stray from his path. But if it is possible to shake his belief system, if it is possible to make him question all that he has based his life on, then he might well be turned from his course.

HONORABLE – nope, that is not a mistake. He has a code of honor; it just is a bit different from the one most people have. But since this man truly believes in his cause, his sense of honor can ultimately be used against him. If he feels he has stained his own honor, he might well destroy himself or betray the cause he will perceive as having betrayed him.

Behavior and Examples of TERRORISTs

Even this darkest of villains can have a comic side. Captain Hook, from **Peter Pan**, has but one goal – to take revenge on Pan, on whom he blames the loss of his hand. But being dedicated to a cause does not necessarily mean you are *good* at it!

Cape Fear was a movie about revenge first made in 1962 and then remade in 1991 with Robert DeNiro playing Max Cady. Cady was a psychotic rapist recently released from prison and determined to take his revenge on the public defender he believes deliberately withheld evidence that would have acquitted him. He gradually steps up his harassment of the lawyer's family, increasing the horror at every turn.

Die Hard II offered two TERRORIST villains – both military men. The traitorous colonel and major both believed they were making a point about America keeping true to anti-communist ideas by aiding the escape of the right wing drug lord. (That villain, unquestionably, was a TYRANT).

HBO's series **Oz** had an exemplary TERRORIST. Vern Shillinger, the leader of the white supremacist Aryan Brotherhood, is a chilling example of someone who honestly believes everything his group stands for. But, in his own sick way, he is an honorable man. He makes no exceptions to his ideals, and hold fast to his position even when it violates his own desires, even his loves. He had his own son killed because the son violated Shillinger's code. BTW – this program, available on DVD, is an ensemble of villains – not really a hero in the bunch – and watching their differences can be quite educational. Take a look at Chris Kellor and Ryan O'Reilly – two very different men – but both DEVILs.

Frollo, from **The Hunchback of Notre Dame,** is a perfect example of how the TERRORIST blinds himself to self examination. He desires Esmeralda. Since he is a man of the cloth who cannot be tempted by any mere woman, then it must be she who is an unholy temptress. Therefore, she must be punished for her sins....

Blind loyalty to a cause is one sure sign of a TERRORIST. Inspector Javert from **Les Miserables** has no room in his soul for compassion, or a sense of perspective. He sees only justice, in its purest form. A TERRORIST would never consider situational ethics.

Proof that a TERRORIST villain need not be violent – the minister and town council in **Footloose**. They believed rock music and dancing were tools of the devil, and led to the tragic death of teens, and therefore, convinced the whole town to outlaw them. And the hero in that movie was able to win because he appealed to the minister's sense of justice, making that "benign" TERRORIST examine his own beliefs.

Alonzo Harris, the ruthless cop played by Denzel Washington in **Training Day** shows how close entwined the TERRORIST/WARRIOR can be. He breaks the law, to catch lawbreakers.

Of course, no discussion of the TERRORIST archetype could be complete without mentioning Darth Vader from **Star Wars** and its sequels. If ever you wonder whether it is true that a villain is the hero of his own story, consider Lord Vader, born Anekin Skywlker. In episodes I and II, Anekin **was** a hero, brave and true – and also, a bit rigid in his beliefs. After his transformation in episode III, and in the episodes IV-VI, Vader, was a steadfast soldier, defending his empire. But he was defeated—*redeemed* actually—when forced to examine what he valued.

Those are the males. Now for the females. Female Villain #1 – The Bitch.

FEMALE VILLAIN #1
THE BITCH

THE BITCH: *the abusive autocrat, she lies, cheats, and steals her way to the top. Her climb to success has left many a heel mark on the backs of others. She doesn't care about the peons around her – only the achievement of her dreams matters. Forget expecting a helping hand from her – she doesn't help anyone but herself.*

The first female villain I will address is a popular one in fiction. The BITCH.

The BITCH is the dark version of the BOSS. (The funny thing about both the BOSS and the CHIEF – it is sometimes hard not to make them seem like villains even when they are the protagonists. That might be because so many of us hate being told what to do, but all four of these archetypes tend to love telling others what to do!)

The BITCH's driving ambition is power, power, and more power.

You know this villain – she's the avaricious stepmother/aunt/sister/etc. who tries to get rid of the true heir so she can control the estate or family company. Or, less insidious (or is it more?), she's the wife and/or mother who had no time for mothering, the woman whose career is more important than relationships, relationships she likely chose to have simply because they advanced her career. This villain might be close to the hero and heroine, but maybe she's a more distant enemy.

Although a BITCH shares much in common with a TYRANT, she also faces issues that he will never endure. A TYRANT might be "forgiven" much of his more extreme megalomania. Ambition is rarely seen as a bad quality in a man, and thus, a TYRANT may at times go to far greater lengths before there is recognition of his dark character. A controlling nature in a woman, however, will often lead to negative responses early on. A BITCH who is open about her need for power is likely to have faced disapproval, revulsion and rejection early on. Of course, what doesn't kill her, makes her stronger....

On the other hand, sexism can serve the BITCH well. Who would believe the gray-haired matron (or the cool blonde with the figure of a model, or whatever vision of a female you consider least threatening) – has a fist of iron, and a heart to match? A BITCH and a TYRANT alike tend to use the system to their own ends, and thus, societal mores often aid to their plans.

As an aside – I am often asked why there are separate archetypes for male and female characters. Of course, since I didn't invent the archetypes, but merely describe the ones that already exist, I cannot give a definitive answer. However, I do have a theory. It is such double standards as the one I describe above that contribute to there being separate archetypes for men and women. Gender impacts society's perception of a character; the character responds (be it through rebellion or submission) to society's perception. This interaction inevitably contributes to the character, resulting in quite different paths for most of the male/female archetypes, and even in some differences in the three pairs of male/female families that do correspond to each other. (BOSS/BITCH–CHIEF/TYRANT; CRUSADER/WARRIOR-TERRORIST/FANATIC; PROFESSOR/LIBRARIAN- EVIL GENIUS/SCHEMER). No one will accuse the TYRANT of being less of a man for his ambition; the BITCH, however, risks constant attack on her "femininity."

Formation of a BITCH

You know the drill by now – the same things that lead to a little girl growing up to be a BOSS, can also push her into the darker world of BITCH. She might have been the petted princess, with servants and parents waiting on her hand and foot. Now she expects such treatment to continue, perhaps amplified with each passing year.

Or she might have led a hand to mouth existence, with every scrap of food hard won. Was her mother also an imperious autocrat? Or was mom a cowering, downtrodden wife, abused by the men in her life? The BITCH believes that power and control equal comfort and safety. No surprise here – her fear is that she will no longer pull the strings, no longer control her own destiny.

So again, when looking to create a backstory for a BITCH villain – think in terms of control. What did she see or experience to make power and control so crucial to her existence? Weapons and vulnerabilities

The Bitch's weapons make her a danger to the H/H.

RESOLUTE – She stays the course. Minor setbacks will not dissuade her. The H/H may win some battles, but she is determined to see the war through to the end.

DOMINEERING – In fact, your average dominatrix might well fit into this category, assuming she has some nefarious plot to thwart the H/H. *Law & Order* had an episode many years ago in which some hard core S & M games led to a death. The villain was a dominatrix who ordered one of her submissives to confess to the crime, leaving her role out of it. Sadly for her, she didn't realize he had a photo of the event. But anyway – giving orders is definitely a trait this archetype will manifest. And her air of command does lead others to obey.

UNFEELING – do not bring a sob story to this woman. She is not interested. Nor is she likely to be swayed to repent of her evil ways simply because of a pair of sad eyes or tears.

Her vulnerabilities are what they use to overcome her.

OBSTINATE - she is not one to admit to making mistakes, which can lead her to stick to a certain path long after a clearer vision would have changed tacks.

SENSE OF SUPERIORITY – the BITCH has a sense of omnipotence. Failure is truly outside her imagination, which can lead her to have unrealistic faith in her own abilities, and a tendency to forget any weaknesses she might actually possess.

Behavior and examples of BITCHs.

The BITCH is capable of any act of cruelty. Keep in mind, however, that she is not likely to use cruelty for its own sake. Instead, it will serve her purpose.

For example, the Wicked Witch of the West is an example of a BITCH who tormented her victims. She drugged them, she sent winged monkeys to terrorize them, she even set fire to the Scarecrow, for example. But not to watch him burn – she wanted Dorothy to give up those Ruby Slippers - slippers that would increase the WWW's power.   Notice that the WWW really wasn't interested in avenging her sister's death – beyond the initial anger, never once did she mention her dead sister. It was all about those powerful shoes.

Cruella Deville, of **101 Dalmatians** was determined to have the coat that would make her the envy of the design world – truly the top of her field. Only problem – the coat would be made of Dalmatians. Is there anything lower than planning to kill puppies?

Ever see the PBS program **I, Claudius**? Livia, wife of Augustus, was a perfect example of a BITCH at her worst. Could anyone keep count of the number of victims who fell at her hand - a meaningless pawn in her quest to control Rome as first wife, and then mother, of the Emperor. She even plotted to become a goddess.

Another royal example is the Evil Queen in **The 10th Kingdom**. Does anyone remember her backstory – the hapless wife of an ineffective man, she jumped at the opportunity to grasp power and riches offered by the fairytale world to which she found a passage.

And still another royal example – the Queen of Hearts, from **Alice in Wonderland**. Off with the heads of anyone who doesn't fall in with her plans. Not difficult to maintain control if you have anyone who even hints at opposition beheaded!

And one more royal example – Cercei, from George R.R. Martin's **Song of Fire and Ice** series, brought to the small screen by HBO in **Game of Thrones**. She lusts for power, and no one, not small boys and certain not the King's Hand, will block her path to control over Westeros.

Of course, a BITCH does not **need** to be murderous.

Think of Sigourney Weaver's character in **Working Girl.** A high-powered executive, she uses her underlings, and takes credit for their ideas to keep her position.

More insidious, but not actual murderous is the chilling example of a BITCH villain that is Nurse Ratched *from One Flew Over the Cuckoo's Nest*. No vast empire at stake there, no piles of money in the offing. But she ruled her tiny kingdom of a mental ward with an iron fist (and no velvet glove, either!

Mommy Dearest may or may not have been an accurate depiction, but it surely showed the dictatorial mother at her worst. It is important to note that "Mommy Dearest" did not seem to have the interests of her child at heart at all – it was a need for control that drove her, not a protective sense. (This difference will be important for distinguishing between the BITCH and another archetype.)

That's the BITCH – Next up is Female Villain #2 - the Black Widow.

FEMALE VILLAIN #2
THE BLACK WIDOW

THE BLACK WIDOW: the beguiling siren, she lures victims into her web. She goes after anyone who has something she wants, and she wants a lot. But she does her best to make the victim want to be deceived. An expert at seduction of every variety, she uses her charms to get her way. Don't be fooled by her claims of love – it's all a lie.

The BLACK WIDOW. . . a movie with that title sums up this villain at her worst – "She mates and she kills."

The BLACK WIDOW uses seduction – whether it is sexual in nature, or something else – to get what she wants. Unlike the BITCH, power and control will not necessarily be her driving motivation, although it could be. More likely, however, what she *really* wants are the goodies that go with power and control. The comfort, the adulation, the luxury –

the security! – that comes with that power. The means to make sure she is never hurt, never vulnerable again. A BLACK WIDOW doesn't really want to rule the universe – she just wants to live like she does.

In fact, of all the archetypes, the BLACK WIDOW is the one who most challenges the "any archetype can do anything" point that I drive home. Because I can think of a few villains who certainly use their wiles to get what they want –and power and control are definitely what they want. Villains like the Borg Queen from **Star Trek: First Contact** and Ursula, the Sea Witch, from **The Little Mermaid** are hard to pin down. Their motivations make them BITCHes. Their actions sure seem to fit BLACK WIDOWs. The sexist part of me suggests that this is another example of male ambivalence toward powerful women – that power in women must involve their sexuality and ability to manipulate men.

But ultimately, the separation can be drawn about how the women perceive themselves. A true BLACK WIDOW will have her identity wrapped up in her femininity. So she might see herself as ruling, but chances are, she'll see a man at her side somewhere. A BITCH would happily rule alone. As would both the Borg Queen, and Ursula.

And, of course, many B LACK WIDOWS are wholly unconcerned about power. She might just want a man. The heroine's man. That makes this villain a frequent character in romance. She's the sultry siren that uses (or tries to use) sex to try to gain the hero. She spreads lies with a silvery tongue to discredit her rival. She wraps herself up to be the woman the hero wants, planning on showing her true colors only when he's caught in her lair.

In fact, in romance, this lady sometimes is a villain who appears only in backstory. The cheating ex-wife or girlfriend, who ignored the noble qualities of the hero, and moved on to a man who offered her more of whatever superficial needs she had – more funny, higher social status, or even a partying lifestyle.

One more thing about the BLACK WIDOW – when Satan shows up wearing in a dress, it will most likely be as a BLACK WIDOW. She is a temptress, and she uses the weakness of her victims to bring about their own downfall.

Formation of a BLACK WIDOW

Somehow, someway, this woman learned early that using her feminine wiles was the key to getting what she wanted. Maybe she followed in her mother's footsteps, watching her mother coax her father into good moods or presents. Or maybe she realized that beauty and charm got her things that the plain and forthright didn't get. Could her sweet appearance have won her approval, while her hardworking mother's washed out appearance earned only scowls?

Or maybe her femininity led to her being hurt or abused, and she resolved to turn it into a weapon.

She developed her cynical attitudes early. As a young girl, she discovered the effectiveness of using her charms to get her way. A smile of promise or a gleam of understanding in her big eyes got her what she wanted - whether from Daddy or the boy next door. Chances are, the adults around her let her know that her appearance was far more important than character or intelligence.

Weapons and vulnerabilities

The Black Widow's weapons make her a danger to the H/H

SEDUCTIVE - A BLACK WIDOW does not need to be beautiful, although they often are.   More important, however, is her ability to be whatever her victim wants. But she does need to be able to determine just what that victim does want.

CLEVER - When things go wrong, the BLACK WIDOW always has a plan B. She sees possibilities, and is accustomed to grabbing at chances.   She's not easily flustered when a situation goes awry.   Assessing the damage, she's smart enough to cover her tracks and wipe away any fingerprints.

OPPORTUNISTIC – she is able to see possibilities, and turn events to her own advantage.

MANIPULATIVE - She has learned that honey catches more flies than vinegar.   Because she's no dummy, she's perfected her honey-making skills, and the seductress sees nothing wrong with fooling people to get her way.

Her vulnerabilities are what they use to overcome her.

CYNICAL - The BLACK WIDOW is jaded. Her distrust of the motives for others can blind her to the true nature of others. This can lead her to make costly misassumptions, and enable the master manipulator to be manipulated.

SELF-PERCEPTION – her whole personality is wrapped up into her appearance, her ability to charm. If an H/H successfully threatens this, they can destroy the BLACK WIDOW.

Behavior and examples of BLACK WIDOWs.

I think more examples of this villain archetype spring to mind than any other. I can help but wonder if the number of examples of this villain archetype in a cultural world dominated by men is a reflection of the male fear of her power.

It wasn't the biggest movie ever, but **Black Widow** certainly summed up the essence of this archetype. The villain, Catherine, played by Theresa Russell, married wealthy men, and then killed them as soon as the willed had been made in her favor. Especially interesting in this movie was Catherine's ability to mold herself into whatever type of woman who appealed to her targeted victim. That chameleon like ability is a major weapon in the BLACK WIDOW's arsenal.

Of course, using feminine wiles to gain riches is a common theme for this villain. Kathleen Turner showed just how sexy, and just how powerful, the BLACK WIDOW could be in Body Heat.

The BLACK WIDOW is a femme fatale. Brigid O'Shaunessey, the villain in **The Maltese Falcon,** lured a man to his death, and dazzles men to keep them from realizing her villainy. And she is stunned – stunned – when Sam Spade does not give her what she wants.

Disney is a great source of memorable villains, and the BLACK WIDOW is one of the most memorable. The Evil Queen, who is furious that **Snow White** could be fairer than she, is a BLACK WIDOW. Note the total absence of concern that the princess might grow up to take the throne. Is there a King. Does the Queen rule in her own right? Just where did that Princess come from, anyway?   Is there another heir? Who knows - The Evil Queen only worries about who is most beautiful. And kills to keep that top spot.

How about a Batman villain? Cat Woman is a wonderful example of the BLACK WIDOW. She tries so very hard to seduce Batman (a short lived TV series **Bird of Prey** suggests she succeeded. This is a good example of how close the line between a villain and a heroine can be. In the movie, was Michelle Pfieffer a villain, or a tragic heroine?

The Old Testament is a source of many, many BLACK WIDOWS – or at least, women who use their charms to persuade men to do bad things. <g>. Eve, who persuaded Adam to eat from the tree of knowledge.   Delilah, who seduced Sampson, and managed to his cut his hair, thereby depriving him of his strength. And the New Testament also provides an example – Salome, who dances to win the head of John the Baptist. Of course, these stories are not long on character development of the villains, so we don't know a lot about motivation – in this case, it is their actions that suggest they fit the BLACK WIDOW archetype.

And of course, since a villain is a secondary character, it is not uncommon for there to be no revelation of his or her backstory. It will help the writer to know that backstory, to be sure that the villain remains consistent, but it is not always necessary for the reader to know it. The writer gets to decide.

Next, female villain #3 – the BACKSTABBER.

FEMALE VILLAIN #3
THE BACKSTABBER

THE BACKSTABBER: the two-faced friend, she especially delights in duping the unsuspecting. Her sympathetic smiles enable her to learn her victims' secrets, which she then uses to feather her nest. Her seemingly helpful advice is just the thing to hinder. Put no faith in her – she'll betray you every time.

Even the SPUNKY KID has a dark side, and that is the BACKSTABBER. I know there is a song about this type of person - the lyrics go something like "she smiles in your face, and all the time, she's tryin' to take your place. The BACKSTABBER!" I looked it up on the Internet, but did not find that song. I did, however, find tons of articles about how to deal with the villain every office has – the BACKSTABBER! That makes me think that just about everyone has met a real, live BACKSTABBER in their lives.

In her darkest form, she can literally be someone who is biding her time before she slides that knife in deep. She might lure the friend to the dark alley, where the thugs await to do the dirty deed. She's the classic double agent. Maybe she's the friendly, helpful Jill of all trades who is quietly gathering information and passing it along. She's the efficient secretary, selling company secrets on the sly to lead to the company's demise.

In her somewhat less dangerous forms, she badmouths the very people who consider themselves her closest friends. Maybe she wants to prevent others from getting promotions. Or she's the jealous friend who tries to break up the romances around her by telling tales on the guys. Or maybe she's doesn't have so nefarious a plan, but is the person who always has the sarcastic remark, the one who can rain on anyone's parade. She's doesn't have to be evil, not even particularly nasty. Just the person who always notices – and comments – on the screw-ups of others.

A well known example, from real life, is someone we'll call Linda. She encouraged Monica to spill all her secrets, never letting on that the conversations were being illegally tape recorded.

Formation of a BACKSTABBER

The BACKSTABBER has probably never been the center of attention. She's not the best and the brightest, not anyone's darling, not the cute one or the smart one or the vamp. Odds are, she's the middle child, the one who is there, but not much noticed. She's the girl next door, and gets exactly the sort of attention the girl next door tends to get. She did fine in school, but probably not great. In other words, this woman has never shone.

And chances are, she isn't even all that unhappy with her lot. Her ambition might well be the status quo, because it is comfortable. But if that status quo is threatened – if her friends look to be moving on without her, if people are getting promoted higher than her, and so on -- well, that might just be what it takes to push the nice kid over the edge.

Of course, the BACKSTABBER could have an abusive background. Maybe she was the target of vicious sarcasm. Maybe she was constantly belittled, so it seems natural to belittle those around her. Or perhaps she saw how her mother advanced by telling tales and putting other people in their place.

Think of what leads a friend to betrayal, and you'll have the backstory for your BACKSTABBER.

Weapons and vulnerabilities

The Backstabber's weapons make her a danger to the H/H.

RELATIONSHIPS – The BACKSTABBER understands people, and knows how to be a great listener. She offers that shoulder to cry on, and listens while life stories are being poured into her ears. She makes connections with people, gains trust, and then is able to use all that she has learned for whatever purpose she might have.

STRONG-WILLED - The BACKSTABBER tends to be a tireless worker, and won't back down easily. Even though she might not be a star, she does know the value of hard work. She won't be easily discouraged from her purpose.

Her vulnerabilities are what they use to overcome her.

INSECURE – In her heart of heart, the BACKSTABBER fears she doesn't measure up. All around her are prettier, smarter, move loved – whatever. A hero or heroine could use this insecurity in two ways.   They could give the BACKSTABBER the attention she desires, thereby winning her to their side. Or they could reaffirm her doubts.

Behavior and examples of BACKSTABBERs

We all remember this brilliant example of the BACKSTABBER - Julia Roberts in **My Best Friend's Wedding** gives every pretence of being happy for her childhood friend, while she's secretly doing her best to sabotage his wedding.

One of the funniest movies ever made is **All of Me**, with Steve Martin and Lily Tomlin. The villain is a sweet young thing who gladly offers up her body so the filthy rich but dying heroine can continue her life. Of course, this villain doesn't really believe the heroine's spirit will enter her own body; she just wants to inherit all that nice money, and what the hey – she's making the poor rich girl die happy. But then when she finds out the mumbo jumbo really works, she fights tooth and nail to avoid living up to her bargain, all the while pretending to be the sweet young thing.

Fans of **Drew Carey** will recognize Mimi as a BACKSTABBER. She shows a friendly face when necessary, but otherwise delights in torturing her office mate, Drew. I think she has even literally stabbed Drew in the back!

The SPUNKY KID roots of the BACKSTABBER were strongly in evidence in **The Truman Show.** Truman's "wife" gamely did her best to get those product endorsements in, even as her "husband" started to suspect the make believe nature of his world.

Remember Sue Ann Nivens, played by Betty White, on the Mary Tyler Moore Show? Ever efficient, always smiling, she managed to say something bad about everyone.

Harmony from **Buffy the Vampire Slayer** only lasted a season (although she showed up in Angel trying to be good), but she certainly showed what happens when a SPUNKY KID becomes an evil vampire. This comic example of the BACKSTABBER tried so hard to be a villain, but she just couldn't seem to pull it off – things kept going wrong. You just knew that this vampire always had runs in her stockings.

But don't be fooled by all these funny examples into thinking that a BACKSTABBER can't be a dangerous. Fans of **24** know that Nina is about as deadly as they come. She repeatedly fools everyone, convinces them to trust her, and then betrays them again.

That's the BACKSTABBER, and that lead us to Female villain # 4 – the LUNATIC.

FEMALE VILLAIN #4
THE LUNATIC

THE LUNATIC: *the unbalanced madwoman, she draws others into her crazy environment. The drum to which she marches misses many a beat, but to her, it is the rest of the world that is out of step. Don't even try to understand her logic – she is unfathomable.*

The LUNATIC can be a chilling villain. Greed, envy, jealousy – those are emotions we do not admire, but can at least understand. But the villain who lives in her own world, who follows a logic of her own making? That kind of unpredictability makes for a wild ride.

We know this villain. She is the obsessed old girlfriend who cannot accept that she and the hero are no longer an item. Or maybe she is the obsessed fan, believing she and the celebrity hero are actually man and wife. Or perhaps she is trapped in some other fantasy, some other dream world, one threatened by the hero or heroine.

Of course, LUNATIC is just a name. This villain need not be actually certifiable. She can be just a bit odd. A tad unconventional. Very funny, even. She doesn't need to sling knives at our hero and heroine. Maybe she just throws a few obstacles in the path of the hero or heroine. She's the secretary who doesn't believe in taking down messages. The aunt who interrupts the passionate tête-à-tête to drag the heroine to an accordion concert. This type of LUNATIC is often a bit ditsy – not malicious, not evil – just not quite all there. This becomes all the more frustrating because the hero or heroine doesn't have the heart to walk away from her. Think of hapless Aunt Clara, from **Bewitched** and you'll see how even a sweet lady can be a villain for literary purposes.

Formation of a LUNATIC

Chances are, the LUNATIC was a bit unusual, even as a child. She definitely saw the world through a different lens than the rest of us. She simply had different goals and hopes than most girls her age. In all likelihood, her parents and siblings were constantly cleaning up her mistakes and explaining away her habit of wandering off. The endearing yet maddening LUNATIC, often found in romantic comedy, often doesn't need much explaining. We all know these people – they just exist. Usually in the family....

But what about when she goes a bit beyond the pale – the LUNATIC who is a more than a bit off – but truly bonkers? As in killing people? Of course, sometimes mental problems run in families. More typically, however, there is a tendency toward a certain problem, but something will have to act as a trigger to make a person actually murderous. Use your imagination to create that trigger. Was something missing from her life – love, affection, a husband, a child - and so she just pretended it existed. Did she think things were fine, but she lost the job, the boyfriend broke up with her, the husband walked out?

Chances are, if the fantasy can be maintained, she'd still be perfectly harmless. It is only when her dream world becomes threatened by reality that she is likely to feel the need to strike out.

Weapons and vulnerabilities

The Lunatic's weapons make her a danger to the H/H.

INGENIOUS – There are advantages to thinking way, way outside the box. The LUNATIC can be amazingly resourceful when she needs to be. Her ability to grasp innovative solutions can help her accomplish her task.

MEDDLING - The LUNATIC has a finger in everybody's pie and loves to stir her friends' and enemies' pots. She's uncontrollably drawn to interfere, whatever the wishes of her victims. She tends to know everyone's secrets, and isn't afraid to make use of them when needed for her own devices.

Her vulnerabilities are what they use to overcome her.

UNDISCIPLINED - Jill of all trades but master of none, the LUNATIC doesn't stick with anything for long. She just might forget all about that grudge she had against the hero or heroine.

RECKLESS – This woman does not necessarily think things through to the logical conclusion. Her plan can fall apart because she acted without taking necessary precautions

Behavior and Examples of LUNATICs

In *Play Misty for Me,* Evelyn Draper seems like a nice enough woman, but she is obsessed with the disc Jockey played by Clint Eastwood. A one night stand turns into much more in her mind, and when she is faced with the truth – that Clint loves another, she does her best to eliminate that rival.

Of course, this type of villain can have a comic side. One of my favorite movies of all time is *Arsenic & Old Lace*. A hapless Cary Grant must deal with a pair of murderously dotty old aunts. Feeling sorry for the poor homeless men who come to their boarding house, these two sweet LUNATICs poison them, to put them out of their misery. Then they have their brother, also mad as a hatter, bury them in the basement.

Lake Placid was one of those half horror/half-comic movies. A serene little vacation community lake is inhabited by a crocodile or two. And then there is the nice sweet lady in town, played by Betty White, who fed a cow to the croc. And when asked if she knows how her husband died, she blithely answers, "Oh, yes. I killed him."

A classic example of a Lunatic is found in **Whatever Happened to Baby Jane?** The former child star often dresses and talks in her little girl way. She torments her helpless sister, feeding her roasted rat for "din-din."

One of my favorite examples of a LUNATIC was the witch in **Robin Hood: Prince of Thieves**. She kept forgetting the spells that would help the Sheriff.

How about the terrifying Alex Forrest in **Fatal Attraction**? She saw eliminating her lover's wife as the best way to fulfill her fantasy that she was the chosen one.

OK – this is the LUNATIC. Next up, female Villain #5 - the PARASITE.

FEMALE VILLAIN #5
THE PARASITE

THE PARASITE: the poisonous vine, she collaborates for her own comfort. She goes along with any atrocity, so long as her own security is assured. She sees herself as a victim who had no choice, and blames others for her crimes. Expect no mercy from her – she won't lift a finger to save anyone but herself.

The PARASITE is the dark version of the PARASITE. Yeah, I know, it is hard to think of the PARASITE as being proactive enough to ever be a villain, but it can be possible. However, I will admit that the nature of this villain is such that it seems unlikely she would be acting alone as a villain. She is more likely to be part of a package deal with some other villain, although there are some exceptions.

The PARASITE goes along to get along. She latches onto to someone, most often a male someone, and sticks with him, whatever. She wants the security offered by that someone, and doesn't worry about the cost to others, or to her own soul. She's the mobster's girlfriend. She's the dictator's mistress. She's the woman who stays with the child- molesting husband or boyfriend.

The PARASITE's villainy tend to be passive. She accepts whatever is going on and makes no effort to stop it. She might even help out if asked or ordered to do so, but she probably wouldn't think of doing it on her own.

However, she can, if cornered, become a force to be reckoned with. She will try to protect the one for whom she credits her comfort, her security, her love, and sometime, just her living. If that means lying to give him an alibi, or accusing someone else of lying about him, that's fine by her. It's a small price to pay to avoid having to go out there and look for another meal ticket.

Formation of a PARASITE

What turn a woman into a complicitor? Well, she'll likely tell you she had no choice – the bad guy forced her into doing whatever it was they did. But the true explanation likely falls into a childhood in which she had little or no power. She learned that submission equaled survival. In creating a women like this, consider whether she observed her mother get by giving in. Of did her mother fight and lose? Did she herself face constant threats, constant dangers? Was she abused physically or emotionally?

Does she believe that any other way of life is even possible?

Weapons and vulnerabilities

The Parasite's weapons make her a danger to the H/H.

INNOCENT-SEEMING – The PARASITE may not actually be innocent, but she is able to convey a sense of innocence or naiveté. And since she likely does belief in her own helplessness, she is able to convince others that she is not responsible for whatever bad thing she helped do.

NON-THREATENING - It's easier for the PARASITE to give in rather than to fight for herself. Her submissiveness can attract men who offer her the kind of protection she wants.

Her vulnerabilities are what they use to overcome her.

IMPRESSIONABLE - She's easily influenced by those around her. The same trusting nature that makes other sympathize with the PARASITE, allows the hero and heroine to use her to defeat the stronger villain. INSECURE - The PARASITE is ruled by her vulnerability, and she often finds herself in trouble because of it. She wants so badly to be loved that she rushes into relationships, hoping and praying that they will work. She's not sure that her opinion is important. In fact, she wonders if maybe she's not important. A hero or heroine can use that insecurity to sway the PARASITE.

Behavior and Examples of PARASITEs

Every gangster movie, every movie about dictators or crime lords, contains a PARASITE or two. They might be arm candy, or maybe they are drudges, but wherever you see evil men of power, you will see these women near by.

Bonnie Parker – the screen versions of this woman portray her as someone in thrall to Clyde. She pretty much gets dragged along into his crime spree, helping out only when it is clear that her survival likely depends on his.

Mallory Knox, from **Natural Born Killers,** is another example of a real PARASITE whose crime spree with a man was made into a movie. She latched on Mickey, and kept with him. Without his influence, she would like never have killed anyone, but she followed his lead.

A classic example of a PARASITE villain is Gertrude, Hamlet's mother. Her husband was murdered, but the new king wanted to marry her, so why protest too much?

Not a movie – but I suspect Eva Braun was a PARASITE.

Next up, female villain #6, the SCHEMER.

FEMALE VILLAIN#6
THE SCHEMER

THE SCHEMER: the lethal plotter, she devises the ruin of others. Like a cat with a mouse, she plays with lives. Elaborate plans, intricate schemes; nothing pleases her more than to trap the unwary. Watch out for her complex designs – she means you no good.

The SCHEMER is a LIBRARIAN gone bad. She has plenty of smarts, and likely an analytical nature. She is accustomed to thinking of herself as smarter than most everyone around her, and she's probably right.

The SCHEMER is a classic sort of villain. The female version of the EVIL GENIUS, she might well be the mad scientist type. Is she plotting to blow up the world? Could she be planning to poison cosmetics so they'll turn the beautiful into the plain? A writer can have loads of fun with this villain – just make sure to create a deep, elaborate plot.

Or maybe she's not quite so dangerous. Does she simply like to show off how smart she is by making others look dumb? Maybe she doesn't even try to make other people look stupid in comparison, it just happens. Maybe she just likes to amuse herself by setting traps for the unwary. Or is she the person who always has to track down the reason for things, analyzing things to death. No one wants a SCHEMER on the team when the meeting drags on.

Formation of a SCHEMER

What makes a nice studious girl turn to the dark side? The SCHEMER likely has lots of reasons to plot. Her brains were far too often a turn off for boys, and later men. She wasn't willing to play dumb to meet their needs, and as a result, she's too often been overlooked.

Or maybe she wasn't taken seriously as the genius she is? Has she been overlooked for some honor, scholarship, opportunity, perhaps because of her gender? Did the boys in her family get sent to college, while she was expected to marry? Was her mother never allowed to show how smart she was? Did the men in the family just assume the little lady had nothing more on her mind than clothes and makeup?

Or did her analytical mind just observe how a bit of planning makes all the difference in the world when it comes to getting what you want? Did he have impetuous parents, who fell victim to the plots of the unscrupulous? Or did she observe how recklessness and spontaneity can lead to disaster?

Weapons and vulnerabilities

The Schemer's weapons make her a danger to the H/H.

PROFICIENT - The SCHEMER gets things done. She doesn't procrastinate, she doesn't dither, she doesn't make excuses. She looks a matter over, decides how best to accomplish the task, and then she does it. The hero and heroine will be hard pressed to find flaws in her theories.

STAID - She isn't one to fool around. Life is work, not a walk in the park. The SCHEMER is not likely to be lured from her plots with sex, drugs or rock and roll.

Her vulnerabilities are what they use to overcome her.

ARROGANCE – she's so sure she is one step ahead of everyone, that she won't always take the needed measures to make certain. The hero and heroine can use her smug self-conceit to delay discovery of the inroads they make on the SCHEMER's plans.

OBSESSIVE - If a thing is worth doing, it is worth doing well. And if it isn't done right the first time, try, try again. And again. The SCHEMER can waste time trying to make her plan work perfectly. A clever hero or heroine can use that perfectionist nature to gain time for their own advantage.

Behavior and examples of SCHEMERs

SCHEMER Marquise de Merteuil inspired no less than three major motion pictures in the last decade or two:

Dangerous Liaisons, with Glenn Close; *Cruel Intentions*, with Sarah Michele Geller; and *Valmont*, with Annette Bening. In all these films, the SCHEMER plotted elaborately to bring about her wicked plans.

Catherine Zeta-Jones was a beautiful SCHEMER in *Entrapment*. She meticulously planned her elaborate theft scheme. Every step in the game was carefully plotted, and only her supreme belief that she had read Sean Connery's character correctly defeated her.

Batman does love those genius villains, and he does have a female version. In *Batman and Robin*, Poison Ivy, the genius chemist, is an example of a SCHEMER. Who else would come up with poisoned lip stick?

A wicked *Star Trek*: *First Contact* villain is found in SCHEMER Borg Queen. Her connection with all the Borg minds makes her a walking computer, capable of analyzing her options in a moment's notice. Faced with defeat by humans, she instantly took the opportunity to travel through time, to conquer Earth at an earlier, more vulnerable time – and elaborate plot that nearly succeeded.

The most recent Bond villainess was a SCHEMER. Miranda Frost, the female villain in *Die Another Day,* was an ice goddess – check the number of times Bond makes reference to her repressed sexuality. She believed that by studying the files on her opponents, she could predict their actions, and thus defeat them.

A SCHEMER can bide her time, and wait decades for her plan to come to fruition. There are many versions of the Arthur legend. In more than a few, Morgan Le Fey's prime motivation is not destroying Arthur. Instead, her target is her rival in magic – Merlin. Imprisoning him in a tree proves herself the more skilled.

Next up, female villain #7 – the FANATIC.

FEMALE VILLAIN #7
THE FANATIC

THE FANATIC: the uncompromising extremist, she does wrong in the name of good. She justifies hers action by her intent, and merely shrugs her shoulders at collateral damage. Anyone not an ally is an enemy, and therefore, fair game. Give up any hope of showing her the error of her ways – she firmly believes you are wrong, wrong, wrong.

The FANATIC has a cause, and nothing will stand in her way. The dark version of the CRUSADER, she possesses a strong sense of right and wrong. It's just that what she views as right might be what you think of as wrong. And chances are, she's willing to do very bad things, provided those things contribute to what she believes is right. Like most villains, she does not view herself as a villain, but she is more convinced than most of her own heroic place in the world.

FANATICs are increasingly popular villains. A female terrorist is likely to fall within this archetype. They do tend to passionately believe their activities are for the greater good, and therefore justified, no matter how horrific the aftermath, or how much innocent individuals suffer from their conduct. A female vigilante also fits the bill here. She takes the law into her own hands.

However, FANATICs are not necessarily violent. A hero and heroine can be obstructed by other means, as well. Characters who file lawsuits or stage protests or take other action to prevent the hero or heroine from achieving their goals also fit this archetypal family, provided the motivation is a dedication to or belief in a particular cause. We see these types of people in the news every day. A person who chains herself to a tree to prevent it being moved to a new location can be a FANATIC – especially if she ignores any compromise solutions. Conversely, the person determined to move the tree might be the FANATIC – absolutely dedicated to the project that requires the tree to go. Or maybe she's the strict nanny, who knows what children "should" do. Villainy is always in the eyes of the hero or heroine, after all!

Often the FANATIC's cause is some far-reaching social issue, but that is not a rule. The FANATIC's cause might be personal. Revenge. Somebody hurt her or hers, and she WILL have justice. We've seen lots of characters like this – obsessed over a past hurt, she is determined to wreak havoc on her target. She'll destroy the family business of the H/H, or frame them for some crime, destroy a career, or maybe even actually kill. All for the sake of getting even. Many horror movies feature a FANATIC seeking vengeance on the townsfolk who either brutalized her, or failed to prevent others from doing so.

Formation of a FANATIC

The FANATIC has a cause of some sort, whether personal or societal. The key to forming the FANATIC is to develop a backstory that explains why this cause means so much to her. If revenge is her motivation, then something bad happened to her, or to someone she loved. She was raped, abused, betrayed, humiliated. If she is a ghost, she was murdered. A family member or other loved one was killed, or ruined financially, or hurt in some other way.

If she has a passionate belief in a cause, then something created that belief within her. Keep in mind that the cause itself might (but need not) be entirely just. It is the FANATIC's methods that make her a villain; her motivation, if less extreme, would be entirely acceptable in a heroine. A political terrorist might have suffered under some regime. An eco-terrorist might have witnessed the rape of the rainforest, or the ruin of the home she loved. A FANATIC anti-abortionist might have regretted the abortion she was talked into, while the pro-choice FANATIC might have witnessed the death of a friend who had an illegal abortion. Whatever the underlying basis, the FANATIC has allowed her passion for the cause to overcome any sense of moderation she might have had. It has become so important, that she allows the end to justify the means – and that usually results in a villain.

Weapons and vulnerabilities

The Fanatic's weapons make her a danger to the H/H.

FAITHFUL – she is a sincere and true believer. Her loyalties will not be easily shaken. She is dedicated to that cause or purpose.

UNYIELDING - while others compromise their beliefs or give up, the FANATIC keeps going. Persistence is a chief virtue for her.

Her vulnerabilities are what they use to overcome her.

RIGID – a narrow minded view often prevents innovation and adaptation. She may stick to a particular mind set, preventing her from seeing the plans of the hero or heroine.

SANCTIMONIOUS - Grimly determined to administer justice, she convinces herself that the end justifies any means. But if her belief system can be successfully challenged – if for example, she discovers her target is not responsible for whatever wrong was done – then her drive might be deflated.

Behavior and examples of FANATICs.

A brilliant example of a FANATIC villain is found in **The Hand That Rocks the Cradle.** The unsuspecting couple does not know that their new nanny blames the wife for the

98

suicide of her own husband, as well as for her miscarriage. As the nanny, she has the means to exact terrible revenge.

Medea demonstrates that this archetype has been with us a long time. When her husband casts her off to marry a wealthy princess, Medea not only kills the bride, but her own children.

Hell hath no fury like a woman scorned. And when the woman is 50 feet tall, she can vent that fury. A film so bad it is fun to watch, ***The Attack of the 50 Foot Woman*** (first made in the fifties, and then remade in the '80's starring Darryl Hannah) featured a woman whose husband not only cheated her, but also used her tale of an encounter with a UFO to have her committed, leaving her nice fortune at his disposal. But once she grows to 50 feet tall, she is able to walk all over everyone who did her wrong.

The Terrorist, a film from India, tells the story of Malli, a young woman who plans to blow herself up as part of a political assassination. While she experiences some doubts, ultimately her commitment to her political cause remains steadfast.

In ***Carrie,*** the mother's religious zealotry leads her to mistreat and abuse her daughter, emotionally and physically.

Now, on to female villain #8, the MATRIARCH.

FEMALE VILLAIN #8
THE MATRIARCH

THE MATRIARCH: *the motherly oppressor, she smothers her loved ones. She knows what's best and will do her best to controls the lives of those who surround her – all for their own good. A classic enabler, she sees no fault with her darlings, unless they don't follow her dictates. Don't be lured into her family nest – you'll never get out alive.*

This one is dedicated to my mom, because just thinking about this villain reminds me of her. <g>

OK, seriously. The MATRIARCH, the dark side of the NURTURER, is one of those villains that you just might have to look hard to find. Not because there aren't scads of them around in literature and film, but because they are so clever at hiding their insidious nature. What's more, their motivation is often so very understandable. After all, a mother bear protects her cubs. Of course, a woman will protect her loved ones.

It is just that the MATRIARCH takes a VERY proactive role when it comes to protection. In fact, she sometimes thinks the best defense is a good offense. She may wrap her child up so tightly in warm clothing that she doesn't even realize the poor kid is dying of heatstroke. Or just plain smothering.

So who is this villain? She's the stage mom, pushing the kid beyond his or her abilities, or even interest. She's the overprotective parent who never lets little Jessica or Jason cross the street alone. Not even when Jessica and Jason are 25 years old.

She's the mother-in-law convinced her daughter-in-law just isn't good enough for her son. She's the grandmother who knows better than mom or dad what those cute grandkids of hers want and need. Asthma medicine? Nonsense, Johnny just needs some good fresh air. No sweets before bedtime? That's just mean — all her kids had candy and cola as a bedtime snack.

Sometimes, she's that voice in our head, murmuring about disappointment, and how she thought we could do better. Maybe she's right. Maybe we just can't do any better. Maybe we should move back home....

Yeah, I know. All of that sounds annoying, not dangerous. And true enough, the MATRIARCH villain often appears in less threatening personas. She's someone's cross to bear, rather than being a major obstacle for hero or heroine to overcome.

Or is she? Actually, the MATRIARCH makes for a pretty terrifying villain. Love is a powerful motivation, able to inspire powerful actions. Maybe she is so determined that you will get that scholarship, she'll kill the other candidates. Or she's so sure that boyfriend of yours is up to no good, she'll buy him off. And if that doesn't work, she'll have him shanghaied. Or destroy his business. Or accuse him of treason. After all, she's doing the right thing – just protecting her baby.

Formation of a FANATIC

It's a great feeling to be needed. To bask in someone's gratitude. To be important in someone's life. The MATRIARCH learned to crave this feeling at an early age. And once she experienced it, she didn't ever want to give it up.

Perhaps she cared for younger siblings, and enjoyed the feeling of responsibility. Maybe a sickly relative depended on her for help and comfort. Maybe she grew up in tight-knit family where mothers cared for children all their lives.

Or maybe she never knew anyone's love. Perhaps she grew up in a household devoid of affection. Was she neglected? Abused rather than cherished? Perhaps a happy family was just a dream for her, one she was determined would come true when she grew up.

If she has certain goals or expectations for her loved ones, are they dreams of her own that were not realized? Will she make sure her children have all the things she wanted, but couldn't have.

Weapons and vulnerabilities

The Matriarch's weapons make her a danger to the H/H.

ALTRUISTIC – well, at least the MATRIARCH is able to **convince** many that she is altruistic. She loves her role as a martyr, and loves the way guilt ties her loved ones to her.

CAPABLE - This woman is a rock in a crisis. The MATRIARCH is great under pressure and keeps her head when those around her are losing theirs. Competent and composed, she's unflappable when the storm hits and unshakable when the rebuilding begins.

Her vulnerabilities are what they use to overcome her.

UNREALISTIC – her view of her loved ones is definitely skewed. She either over or underestimates their capabilities.

OBSESSED – She is so obsessed with "protecting" her loved ones, that the clever hero or heroine can use that obsession to their own advantage. Just convince the MATRIARCH that her plan actually harms the one she loves, and she'll give in.

Behavior and examples of Matriarchs

In *Serial Mom,* the Matriarch merrily kills anyone who stands in the way of her children's success. You could think to yourself, "oh, that's just a movie, it could never happen in real life."

Except, of course, that another movie was made depicting the actual event of a soccer mom in Texas plotting to kill the mother of her daughter's cheerleading rival, hopping the distress would cause the girl to fail the cheerleading trials. *The Positively True Adventures of the Alleged Texas Cheerleader- Murdering Mom* played the story for laughs, but Wanda Holloway was convicted of attempted murder.   At least one report of the story mentions that when she was a teen, her strict father refused to allow her to be a cheerleader.

In most version of Cinderella I've seen, the Wicked Stepmother's motivation isn't really played up.   But we do know she wants one of her daughter's to marry the prince, and is just fine with standing in the way of true love to accomplish that task. She favors her own children over the step child.

Kathy Bates provided a chilling example of someone who is entirely willing to cause **Misery** to a loved one, under the guise of caring for that loved one.

The mother in **Wild at Heart** is murderously protective of her little (teenaged) girl. When the girl runs off with her boyfriend, Mama gets very upset, and tries to have the boy killed.

Imagine Mary Tyler Moore as a villain?   Yes, it happened in   **Ordinary People.**   She was not a murderous villain, but this movie shows the psychological impact of maintaining the fiction of a happy family, instead of trying to understand why the family isn't happy.

Keep in mind that a villain need not be evil, evil, evil. Sometimes, they are just annoying – they antagonize the hero or heroine.   Think of the mother in **My Big Fat Greek Wedding,** or Debbie Reynolds as Albert Brooks's   **Mother**. Does anyone else remember the TV show "**My Mother the Car**?

And there you have it – the sixteen villain archetypes. Try your hand at the exercises to begin crafting your dynamic villain!

EXERCISE ONE
CHARACTER MOTIVATION

Motivation is a crucial aspect of characterization – the character must always have a reason for his or her conduct. All of a character's goals – whether the major, overarching goal in the story, or the more immediate goal of an individual scene, must relate back to that motivation.

Motivation generally develops in a character's backstory. While a prologue sometimes reveals the events in a character's life that lead them to a particular desire, more typically, those events will be revealed in small dribbles here and there. But even though the reader may never read the whole scene or scenes that develop the character, the writer should have a clear picture of those events that build the character's psyche.

Now, imagine that a villain wants to become the CEO of the company belonging to the hero or heroine. I won't give you any more detail than that.

Your assignment – in one paragraph, explain why your villain wants that company. Choose any archetype. But then choose another, and do it again. Ultimately, try moving through each of the villains, to gain an understanding of the importance of motivation in building a character.

Go ahead and tell rather than show, if you must. Chances are, this would never show up in the book itself. But do think about how the differences in the villains' experiences would influence the battles the hero and heroine would face with the different villains.

If a contemporary setting like this does not suit you, you may change that basic structure to fit the genre or setting with which you are most comfortable. The villains want the ranch, or the space station, or the estate, or whatever.

EXERCISE TWO
PHYSICAL APPEARANCE

Most character workshops focus on the development of the character. It is very important for a writer to know and understand her characters. And using archetypes is also geared to the creation of characters.

But once a writer knows that character, he must be able to convey that character to the reader. Thus, part of characterization is showing, rather than telling, character. There are several ways to show character to the reader, beginning with physical description.

So, after completing Exercise 1, you understand how backstory helps to create the character. Now you are ready to write a paragraph or two describing the physical appearance of each of your villains.

Sound easy? Ah, but there is a catch to this.

You must take two villains, and turn them into identical twins. That's right – for each pair, their height, hair and eye color, bone structure, facial features, shoe and hand size, and general proportions are all identical. So what do you do to show how the two villains differ?

That may seem a bit daunting, but think about it. You know many men in the real word who are 6 feet tall and dark haired. That really doesn't tell you anything about personality, does it? But what if he is 6 feet tall, and wears cowboy boots that add another two inches? Or goes barefoot whenever possible? Or wears heavy military books? Or ratty sneakers? Or polished loafers?

And what if that dark hair is cut in a military style? Or worn in a long pony-tail down his back? Or worn long and loose?

I think you are getting the idea. In describing these two villains, consider how their different personalities would result in different appearances – including hair style/cut, facial expression, manner of dress, body build, and general demeanor. Take it a bit further if you like, and consider what your characters' homes look like, what their workspaces are like, what kind of vehicle they use, and so on. Environment is part of physical description, and it says a great deal about personality.

After you've done this with a pair of villains of one gender, choose two of the opposite gender. Remember -- identical twins.

Lots of thin blondes in the world (being a far-from-thin brunette, I always pick on thin blondes!), but they aren't exactly interchangeable. Short or long hair? Heavily made up or fresh faced? Glasses or not? Overtly trampy clothes or loud frumpiness? Superficially demure with an underlining sexuality? No nonsense, buttoned up to the collar style? Spike heels or Birkenstocks? Think about how personalities influence personal choices.

Have fun!

EXERCISE THREE
PERCEPTIONS OF OTHER CHARACTERS

Another way to show a character's personality is to reveal how other characters see him. Your readers will learn about these attitudes and opinions through the interaction of other characters with the villain, and also, when other characters discuss the villain.

Are people afraid of him? Do they talk about her behind her back? Has everyone always been disappointed in him? Have they always excluded her?

An exercise I use in the workshops I give is to ask participants to imagine their character coming home and checking the answering machine. I give a list of likely types to leave messages. The message left should give an idea of what the person thinks of the villain.

So, let's give that a try here.   Tell what messages (be brief) a character you envision as any of the villain archetypes might receive from the following persons:

Mother

Recently married sister

An old school friend

Former fiancé

Younger (but adult) brother

Hero or heroine

When you have finished, start anew, using another villain archetype.

And here is a twist on this.   The exercise above assumes the villain will hear the message.   Thus, the speaker does not care if the villain knows about this opinion.   So imagine a different scenario:

The villain is at a party, and while lurking behind a potted plant, eavesdrops on a conversation about – you guessed – our villain. What does she or he hear?

EXERCISE FOUR
INTROSPECTION

Ok - you've seen appearance/environment used for characterization, and you've seen how other character's perceptions can be used for characterization. The third way to show characterization is introspection. This is actually the way that is probably most used—perhaps even overused at times (mostly because it sometimes seems as though introspection is the only characterization method used in a book). But while I think we are tempted to rely a bit too much on introspection, it is still an important way of showing who the character is.

Now, let's get inside our villains' heads! How do different archetypes think?

Your villain has just been fired from his/her jobs. The bosses each just walked on to the job first thing that morning, went up to the villain and said, "You're fired!" No explanation. Just "you're fired."

For the next hour or so, what goes through your villain heads?

Remember - this is introspection. Don't worry about actual action--- just thoughts.

Once you try this with one villain archetype, try it with another. The thoughts are different, aren't they?

Have fun.

EXERCISE FIVE
WORDS AND DEEDS

Ok – we've had exercises on how villains look, how others view their personalities; how they react internally under stress. Now it is time for them to speak (or act)!

A character's actions are truly the greatest indication of the personality. What we actually do says more about us than anything else. The choices we make – that defines character.

So imagine your villain is driving down the road. All at once, s/he is rear-ended by another vehicle.

What does your villain say? What, if anything, does s/he do?

When you finished putting one villain in a wreck, try it with another.

Enjoy!

ABOUT THE AUTHOR

Tami Cowden wanted to be a writer since she was a teenager. After 20 some years of thinking how great life would be when she was a writer, it occurred to her that to reach that goal, she'd actually have to put words down on paper. So she starting writing, and received the Individual Achievement in Fiction Award from America Mensa, Ltd. for her first short story. Tami is also one of those obnoxious people who sold on her first try, earning $500 for a 1000 word story. But don't hate her – the editor who bought her story quit shortly thereafter, and Tami has never sold to that magazine again. But she has sold more than 20 other short stories since, and her stories have appeared in three award nominated anthologies, *Love Triumphs, Love Mystifies and Love Sizzles.* Her first novel, *Cruising for Love*, winner of RWA's Golden Heart, was released by Avalon Books.

Tami is the coauthor of *The Complete Writers Guide to Heroes and Heroines: Sixteen Master Archetypes,* a guide to characterization for writers. Tami has presented writing programs on characterization, plotting and scene building at more than 100 writing conferences and retreats, as well as online. A lawyer by day, she is now working on a mystery series about a divorce lawyer who inherits a Las Vegas wedding chapel.

CPSIA information can be obtained at www.ICGtesting.com
Printed in the USA
LVOW080950041112

305759LV00001B/46/P